MW00942966

THE NEHEMIAH EFFECT:
ANCIENT WISDOM FROM THE
WORLD'S FIRST AGILE PROJECTS

BY
TED KALLMAN, PMP, CSM,
CERTIFIED SCRUM PROFESSIONAL
ANDREW KALLMAN, MBA, PMP,
CSM, CERTIFIED SCRUM PROFESSIONAL

The Nehemiah Effect
Ancient Wisdom from the World's First Agile Projects
by Ted Kallman, PMP, CSM,
Certified Scrum Professional,
Andrew Kallman, MBA, PMP, CSM,
Certified Scrum Professional

Printed in the United States of America

ISBN 9781628719161

www.xulonpress.com

TABLE OF CONTENTS

PREFACE

"The only thing that is permanent is change."
Lao Tzu (Laozi)

"Computer processing speed will double and its cost reduced every 18 months."
Moore's Law

"Bandwidth will double and its cost reduced a little faster than computer processing speed." Burrus' Law

"Computer storage capacity will double and its cost reduced every 12 months." Nobody's law, but a current fact

We all know change is inevitable and as prudent planners and managers we take steps to deal with the certainty of its occurrence. We try to anticipate and then plan for how we will navigate the risks that change creates. One of the recent management frameworks created to deal with the need to quickly adapt and adjust in today's fast paced and change rich environment is called Agile. In 2001 a document was created to begin to codify this new approach, "the Agile Manifesto."

Ted Kallman has been leading organizations and businesses for the past 30+ years using a simple leadership framework. It began as a grouping of tools and methods that we referred to as "the Model."

Ted Kallman and Andrew Kallman have refined and grown "the Model" together during the past two decades into what we now call the **Unified Vision Framework** (**UVF**), a methodology agnostic, and Business Agile leadership approach at the executive or Enterprise and project level of organizations in Europe, Asia and the USA. In other words, we have successfully implemented our framework in organizations that were using Agile, Scrum, Lean, Six Sigma, Theories of Constraints, Balanced Scorecard, Waterfall and other homegrown methodologies. We tracked the Value-add of using the **UVF** for many of these organizations over a 10-year period of time. The total increased revenues, cost savings and risk mitigation totaled in excess of $100 million.

The underlying management approach or method does not matter.

The **UVF** cuts across methodology and culture. When properly engaged, it has effectively improved the bottom line for businesses and non-profits worldwide regardless of the management style. It has made them more Agile. For the past few years, we have applied the **UVF** in the new and emerging

Scrum/Agile environments, and yes, the **UVF** has made Agile even more Agile.

Solomon stated in the ancient Hebrew texts, "there is nothing new under the sun." Even though we live in a time of accelerated change this is still true today. For example, a clockwork creation of Pierre Jaquet-Droz that he made when he was around 50 years old in the 1770's was potentially the world's first programmable mechanical computer. If you search YouTube for "Pierre Jaquet-Droz" plus "automaton" you will find a clip from BBC for the device that is absolutely stunning. But, the amount of time it took to program this early word processor in order to create the output was extreme. Where today for example, we can use Word and type the same text and print it in a matter of seconds.

We found an example from the 1800's where the Prussian military conducted the modern world's first retrospective. A White Paper on this can be viewed on our website (www.pmobrothers.com) titled, "The Prussians are Cunning." The framework described in that white paper shows that the Prussians used **VSPT** (Vision, Strategy, Projects and Tactics). We will look at the **VSPT** Model in more detail later in this book. We draw your attention to this because processes and tools that work because they are based on sound principles will continue to work regardless of the speed at which our world is changing. We may have to adjust and adapt how we utilize them but they will be beacons pointing us toward success.

To demonstrate the speed at which change is occurring in our world, we looked at the October

2013 statistics for online activities from comScore.com, a company that collects and analyzes online data. It showed Pinterest with 43 million unique visitors for the month of October. Twitter came in at 65 million. And Facebook had 178 million. LinkedIn had 184 million. What's interesting about these statistics is that none of these companies existed 11 years ago. Pinterest started in 2010, Twitter in 2006, Facebook in 2004 and LinkedIn in 2003. They are all relationship-based companies that are thriving in the new knowledge economy. According to Buckminster Fuller's 'knowledge doubling curve' up until 1900 knowledge doubled every 100 years. By the end of World War II knowledge was doubling every 25 years. We now see knowledge doubling every 12 months. Digital Information doubles every 11 hours.

The speed at which things are changing is disrupting and transforming every part of our culture and economy. If you approach the new economy with old world tools based on unsound principles or which cannot adapt to the new reality you will be left out.

We have been asked numerous times during the past 15 years to write a book that shares how the **UVF** works and how to implement it. This book is the culmination of that effort. We have set it up in four parts.

Section One, *The Basics*, defines the **Nehemiah Effect** as we journey with you through the basics of Agile and it takes a quick look at some of the challenges facing Agile methodologies.

Section Two describes the *Elements of Successful Agile*. Jeff Sutherland, co-founder of Scrum, shared in the Keynote address at the 2013 Scrum Gathering in Las Vegas that only 42% of Agile projects are successful as compared to Traditional/Waterfall's success rate of 14%. Sutherland pointed out that even bad Agile is better than good Waterfall. If we accept these statements as true, then Agile is better than Waterfall. In our experience, all of these will increase their rate of success when combined with the **UVF**.

Section Three demonstrates *Nehemiah's Success Using Agile Principles*. Nehemiah utilized almost all of the elements and artifacts of Agile principles (and the **UVF**) 2,500 years ago with amazing success. We intersperse our comments in the original text so that you can follow Nehemiah's report back to the Project's Product Owner, the king of Babylon.

Section Four illustrates how to do *Enterprise Agile – Using the UVF at the PMO Level and Above to Scale to 50k team members and More*. Scaling Agile is one of the toughest challenges facing CEOs and organizational leaders across the globe since the cultural changes necessary to scale Agile requires significant commitment to the transformation that can take as long as five to seven years to implement successfully.

Leadership will always be a key **Driver** in any successful transformation project. As accelerated change and technological forces converge on over-worked and stressed out employees good leadership combined with effective tools become even more important.

Josh Bersin demonstrates this truism in a blog post on LinkedIn that states, "Deloitte's 'Human Capital Trends 2014 found that the top two people issues facing organizations in 2014 are leadership and retention." It is near impossible to lead well without a clear **Vision**. If that **Vision** is not clearly **Defined** and communicated down to the transactional task level then you risk being a statistic on the 'failed project' side of the project management ledger. The frustration generated by this lack of clarity can contribute to your best people leaving. The **UVF** deals with both of these issues, leadership and retention, by applying ancient wisdom to today's biggest problems with stunning results.

As our investment friends tell us often in their radio ads, past results are not a predictor of future benefits. The rapid change environment of the 21st century makes this even truer. This is why the right tools and the right focus on a compelling **Vision** are more important now than ever before.

A phrase we have often heard over the years is; *"we never have problems, we only have opportunities."* This is true in many respects and it helped our brother Dan keep a positive, solutions-based focus for the software development teams that he led at a Fortune 500 company during the 1990's. The continuous success of the projects Dan has led over the years speaks to the wisdom of adopting this "can do" attitude.

However, the speed and force of any given change or circumstance that is thrust upon you may not allow any time for adaptation (or turning the problem into an opportunity). If an overwhelming force, like a Tsunami, wipes out your home or business, you may find opportunities for leadership and heroism and even lessons learned. But, at the point it hits, it is a problem.

We are now living at the convergence of **technological** and **knowledge growth** never experienced by mankind at any time in our history. This is not change management or incremental adjustments to existing plans. This is disruptive, transformational change that requires new mindsets and new tools combined with seasoned ancient wisdom.

Welcome to the **Nehemiah Effect**.

SECTION 1 –
THE BASICS

CHAPTER 1

THE NEHEMIAH EFFECT

Ne·he·mi·ah ef·fect
\\⬚nē-(h)⬚-⬚mī-⬚\ \⬚fekt\
noun
1. The stunned reaction of seasoned observers to a project result.
Synonyms: Ancient Agile, Business Agile, Enterprise Agile, Scaled Agile,

Nehemiah indeed stunned the people of his day with a project result that no one thought was physically possible to accomplish. As a matter of fact, we just got off the phone with a consultant in South Africa who was not aware of the story and we had asked him how long would it take to rebuild a wall that big at that time in history? His response was "years with tons of immigrant labor." His response when we told him 52 days was … wow, that's amazing!

It is our understanding, belief and experience that projects today can have the same level of success and response by applying the principles that Nehemiah utilized.

In the following pages we will be looking at modern Agile principles that were effectively applied by this leader 2,450 years before "Agile" would become a buzzword in the business community around the world. Large-scale building projects in Nehemiah's day were not short-term endeavors, for example:

- The rebuilding of the Second Temple at Jerusalem took from 535 BC all the way to 516 BC (with the majority of the work being done during the 522 – 516 BC time frame since the original project got derailed by the Samaritans shortly after the original approval for the project was given by the king).
- The final touches to the Temple by Ezra took 13 years and cost over $15 million dollars to complete the work.

The starting point for Nehemiah's project was not a pretty picture:

- The walls were broken down
- The gates were burnt
- The people were defeated
- They had enemies opposing them and successfully frustrating their efforts

By any reasonable standard of estimation or measurement, not one person would have predicted that Nehemiah's project could or would be completed, let alone in only 52 days. But, that is exactly what happened: a stunned response … a Nehemiah Effect.

Here is how the Bible records the result of the first scaled Agile project in history in Nehemiah 6:15:

"So the wall was completed on the twenty-fifth of Elul, in fifty-two days."

Further, in verse 16 it states:

"When all our enemies heard about this, all the surrounding nations were afraid and lost their self-confidence, because they realized that this work had been done with the help of our God."

Basically, all of Nehemiah's enemies were standing off in the distance and looking at the tangible results of Nehemiah's project. We can hear them saying something similar to our consultant friend from South Africa, wow, "look what they've accomplished, surely their God must be with them." The enemies that wanted to stop the project and who had successfully done so for decades were defeated.

This was an over-the-top result by any measure that the world has to offer. That should be music to any business leader, ScrumMaster or project manager's ears.

Agile methodologies are easy to understand. They are not easy to implement. A recent Agile study by Voke, Inc. titled "Market Snapshot: Agile Realities"[1] showed that 64% of the companies attempting to transition from Waterfall to Agile found it much more difficult than they expected. Simple is seldom easy. In fact, it is not easy. The speed at which you can change Culture is the biggest obstacle to success.

Nehemiah gives us a roadmap of how to accomplish an impossible goal using Business Agile principles. We believe that Nehemiah's example will help lead you and your organization to achieve a Nehemiah Effect.

Chapter 1 Action Steps

1. Take a minute to identify and write down an outcome or result that will stun your current stakeholders in a positive way.
2. What is the success rate for projects in your organization?
    a.   Why?
3. What can you do, today, that will increase your project's chances of success?

CHAPTER 2

WHAT IS AGILE? AND, WHY SHOULD I CARE?

"The Gartner 2012 advisory on application development to all IT senior management is: Business users are losing patience with old-school IT culture. Relationships are tense and resentful. Legacy systems and practices impede agility. Bottom line—GET AGILE. Adopt a product perspective. Say goodbye to waterfall. Improve cross-competency collaboration. Launch a deep usability discipline. Start a technical debt management program."[2] *Dr. Jeff Sutherland*

Some years ago a new type of project management methodology appeared on the scene, collectively known as "Agile." But, as we stated in the Preface, there really isn't anything new under the sun. Solomon wrote this many millennia ago:

"That which has been is that which will be,
And that which has been done is that which
will be done. So there is nothing new under
the sun." Ecclesiastes 1:9

We don't want to pop the modern Agile movement's bubble, but they weren't the first practitioners of Agile methodologies. The builders of the Tower of Babel understood Business Agile principles over 4,000 years ago and Nehemiah clearly understood and used these principles 1,500 years later (almost 2,500 years before the Agile Manifesto was published on the web in 2001). Speaking of the manifesto, let's start there for a better understanding of what Agile is all about today:

"We are uncovering better ways of developing
software by doing it and helping others do it.
Through this work we have come to value:
Individuals and interactions *… over processes and tools*
Working software *… over comprehensive documentation*
Customer collaboration *… over contract negotiation*
Responding to change *…over following a plan*
That is, while there is value in the items on the
right, we value the items on the left more."[3]

And in addition to the manifesto there are twelve principles behind the Agile Manifesto (that Agile practitioners generally agree to follow) which are:

1. "Our highest priority is to satisfy the customer through early and continuous delivery of valuable software.
2. Welcome changing requirements, even late in development. Agile processes harness change for the customer's competitive advantage.
3. Deliver working software frequently, from a couple of weeks to a couple of months, with a preference to the shorter timescale.
4. Business people and developers must work together daily throughout the project.
5. Build projects around motivated individuals. Give them the environment and support they need, and trust them to get the job done.
6. The most efficient and effective method of conveying information to and within a development team is face-to-face conversation.
7. Working software is the primary measure of progress.
8. Agile processes promote sustainable development. The sponsors, developers, and users should be able to maintain a constant pace indefinitely.
9. Continuous attention to technical excellence and good design enhances agility.
10. Simplicity—the art of maximizing the amount of work not done—is essential.

11. The best architectures, requirements, and designs emerge from self-organizing teams.
12. At regular intervals, the team reflects on how to become more effective, then tunes and adjusts its behavior accordingly."[4]

OK, sounds good. Why all the fuss and why should I care?

Primarily, in today's competitive environment, everyone is being asked to do more, with less, faster and at a quality level equal to, or better than, what we've traditionally **Delivered** in the past. This is true across the entire business, Non-Governmental Organization (NGO) and Non-Profit spectrum, but it is particularly true in software development where new products and ideas are hitting the market at an increasingly rapid pace. If you aren't getting faster or more Agile, you are the path of loss, insignificance or organizational death. Agile is a tool that is proven to generate all of the above named results and benefits.

We use the terms "Agile" and "Scrum" interchangeably throughout this book because 80% of all current Agile projects are either Scrum or a blend of Scrum and other Agile methodologies (i.e. XP, Kanban, etc.).

When we use the term "**Business Agile**" we are specifically referring to our proprietary model, the **UVF** since it is a methodology neutral leadership framework that works within any existing organizational structure to make it more Agile and effective.

We have used it with great success in both Agile and traditional environments.

Project leaders need to be very careful because if the only tool that they have is a hammer, then soon everything will look like a nail. Agile methodologies are only one of many tools available to a ScrumMaster or a project manager. A very recent example is a PMP certified project manager who was tasked with **Delivering** a small project in a short time frame with a team of one other person. His CIO and PMO both stated that it would not be possible to accomplish the task within the time frame. He used a Scrum format to work with the programmer and the Stakeholders and **Delivered** the project with time to spare and on budget.

The following is a list of some of the most common project management and software development methodologies and tools in use today:

- Pure Waterfall
- Practical Waterfall
- "V" Model
- Short Cycle "iterative" Waterfall
- Spiral Development Model
- Lean / ToC (Theories of Constraints, including ideas like Lean, Six Sigma, Kanban, etc.)
- SED (Staged Evolutionary Development), *sic*
- FDD (Feature Driven Development)
- RUP (IBM's Rational Unified Process)
- DSDM (Microsoft's proprietary system)
- ASD (Adaptive Software Development)
- Scrum

- XP (Extreme Programming)

This list of Software Development Life Cycles (SDLCs) are roughly sorted in order from command-and-control at the top (Waterfall) down to self-organizing Agile methodologies (Scrum & XP) at the bottom. We list only software related methods here because Agile began in the software development space and is still best known for operating within those walls.

A fully trained project manager with some experience and certification in at least one traditional and one agile methodology like Scrum should not only understand but know when and how to best use each of these SDLCs.

Our view of the continuum of project management methodologies looks like this:

Project Management Methodology Continuum

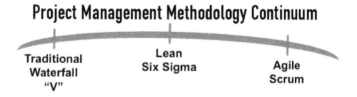

Traditional	Lean	
Waterfall	Six Sigma	Agile
"V"		Scrum

All of the graphic images in this book are available on our website.

Of all of the Agile methodologies at the right of the continuum, Scrum is one of the most well known and easiest to understand, so we'll go through a brief introduction to Scrum.

For each of these methodologies, they all fall under the umbrella of **Vision** and for items relating to **Vision** we will be integrating the picture of the continuum with many of the other Figures throughout this book.

Jeff Sutherland in "Software in 30 Days" describes Scrum as "a framework for managing complex work, such as software development. It is very simple consisting of three roles, three artifacts and five events (i.e. ceremonies). Scrum binds them together with rules of play."

3 Roles	3 Artifacts	5 Events

• ScrumMaster
• Product Owner
• The Team
  (Developers)
	• Product
	  Backlog
	• Sprint Backlog
	• Increment
	  (Sprint)
		• Sprint Planning
		• The Sprint
		• Daily Scrum
		• Sprint Review
		• Retrospective

It is important to maintain clear separation of roles when doing Agile. In order to preserve those boundaries, clear **Definitions** are needed. As we understand Scrum, the following are the three **Defined** roles:
- The **ScrumMaster** – is a facilitator of the daily 15-minute stand-up meetings that the team has every day and works to remove the impediments preventing the team from achieving their goals.
  - The ScrumMaster is only one individual (the SM cannot and should not fulfill multiple roles on the same team) and

help resolve impediments, keep the team in the zone and keep the Scrum artifacts visible.
- ○ They are responsible for shielding the team from external interference, enforcing time boxes, keeping the separation of roles, facilitating the Scrum process and maintaining team self organization.
- ○ The ScrumMaster can help the Product Owner with release planning and advocate for improved engineering practices. A ScrumMaster has no authority.
- ○ The ScrumMaster and the Product owner should use the **UVF's 4D Model**, or a similar methodology, to clarify **Definition** and **Distill Agreement** among all stakeholders prior to attempting to **Deliver** on the product backlog items for the a Sprint.
- The **Product Owner** – is sometimes called a "Product Manager" in some organizations and is the voice of the Customer (or end user).
- ○ The Product Owner is only one person (just like the ScrumMaster, the PO cannot and should not fulfill multiple roles on the same team) and this person owns **Product Vision**.
- ○ One of their key value-adds is constantly reprioritizing the Product Backlog at the beginning of each Sprint and negotiating

the current Sprint's goals and Sprint Backlog with Scrum Team.

○ The Product Owner is responsible for sorting, stocking, ordering, grooming and prioritizing the Product and Sprint Backlogs (the list of all of the items that will be used to create the potentially shippable product, service or result).

♦ The Product Owner is responsible for Release Planning and Product Management.

○ They synthesize the interests of all Stakeholders, including the Scrum Team, and are responsible for Project ROI.

○ The Product Owner is the final arbiter of requirement questions arising from the Scrum Team and accepts or rejects each product increment at the end of the Sprint.

○ In the **UVF's** Business Agile methodology, we continuously filter these activities through prism of the company's **Vision**.

• The **Scrum Team** – all team members are considered Developers regardless of skill set, area of focus or expertise.

○ The **Scrum Team** is a cross-functional, autonomous and self-organizing group that is held responsible for the commitments made for each Sprint. Ideally they are co-located with a team size in the range of 7 (+/- 2) members.

- ° No one (not even the Scrum Master) tells the Development Team how to turn Product Backlog items (i.e. User Stories) into Increments of potentially releasable functionality.
  - ♦ All teams are self-organizing and self-governing.
- ° All team roles are considered interchangeable.
  - ♦ It is really important to note that the *Scrum Handbook*[5] by Sutherland and Schwaber points out that people understand that Scrum recognizes no titles for Scrum Team members other than Developer, regardless of the work being performed by the person; there are no exceptions to this rule.
  - ♦ Sutherland and Schwaber go on to point out that individual Scrum Team members may have specialized skills and areas of focus, but accountability belongs to the Scrum Team as a whole.
- ° Finally, Scrum Teams do not contain sub-teams dedicated to particular domains like testing or business analysis.
  - ♦ In other words, follow the rules for Scrum at the project level as set forth in Southerland and Schwaber's handbook and you'll do fine.

Even today, when writing this chapter, we reviewed portions of the Scrum Alliance website along with the *Scrum Handbook*, and found that response of the Scrum experts regarding Scrum roles did not align with pure Scrum methodology as outlined in the handbook.

Scrum starts by creating a list of **Product Backlog Items** (can be "User Stories" or other types of backlog items) to capture the Business Requirements for a project. Essential to Agile success is simplification and clarity of **Definitions**. It is critical to narrow product scope to only the most essential items needed to **Deliver** the **Vision**.

In his book *Agile Product Management with Scrum*[6] Roman Pichler states *"when it comes to product vision, less is more. The vision should be brief and concise. It should only contain information critical to the success of the product. The blockbuster products in Lynn and Reilly's ten-year study have no more than six product attributes, for instance (2002). The product vision is not, therefore, a feature list, nor should it provide unnecessary detail. Agile project management expert, Jim Highsmith, explains 'coming with 15 or 20 product capabilities or features proves to be easy. Selecting the 3 or 4 that would incent someone to buy the product is difficult.'"*[7] Pichler additionally states, *"starting with an overly long and complex product backlog makes it difficult to create focus and to prioritize items. Use the product idea or vision to guide your efforts. Focus only on what is critical and do not worry about the rest for now. Resist the temptation to add too much detail too quickly. Items are detailed progressively according to their priority."* [8]

In other words, the **Vision** and clear **Definitions Drive** the Product Backlog; and, the **Product Backlog** should encompass the entire **Product Vision**.

The **Sprint Backlog** is a set of ordered product backlog items that are chosen and used by the team during the 2 – 6 week Sprint (iteration) in which a potentially shippable product, service or result is created by the team. On Scrum Alliance's website they have the following illustration for how Scrum works:[9]

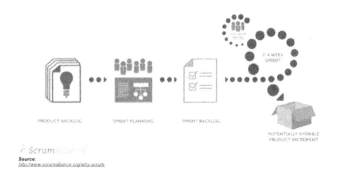

PRODUCT BACKLOG   SPRINT PLANNING   SPRINT BACKLOG

POTENTIALLY SHIPABLE PRODUCT INCREMENT

2-4 WEEK SPRINT

ScrumAlliance
Source:
http://www.scrumalliance.org/why-scrum

Throughout this book, we will be demonstrating Scrum, using the **UVF's 4D Model** (**Define, Distill, Deliver and Drive**), as follows:

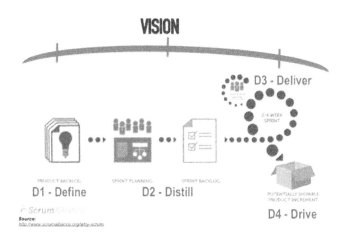

The **4D Model** is a Business Agile iterative process that we have been using for the past two decades on all types of projects across the world. While this looks like a simple and straightforward process, Agile and Scrum techniques require a higher level of team discipline and professionalism than if the project team were to use a more traditional methodology to try to get their project done. The **UVF**, when applied correctly, makes any methodology, including Scrum, more Agile and effective.

The **4D Model** organizes the plan and **Drives** success. It is the compelling core of the **UVF** because without the iterative operation of this process the Purpose / Mission / **Vision** can remain unclear and operational focus and **Delivery** scattered. Continuous reminders of the Purpose / Mission / **Vision** are needed because we are working with people and, as we will demonstrate below in the section on "Why Simple is Better," people forget.

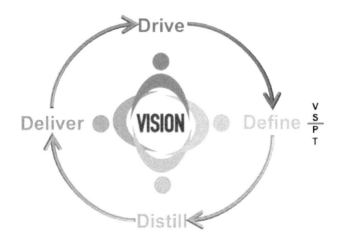

The **4D Model** is a business leadership framework that strengthens and accelerates any (project management) methodology to which it is applied.

Everyone agrees that all organizations are being asked to do more, with less, faster and at a quality level equal to, or higher than, what has been traditionally **Delivered** in the past. Scrum and other Agile methodologies have clearly demonstrated a positive momentum toward these objectives. It is best summed up by Jeff Sutherland, co-creator of Scrum, when he blogged that "the tipping point has been reached and the choice is now to get Agile or get outsourced," as stated in our quote at the beginning of this chapter.

The **UVF** has been constructed using ancient wisdom applied to the modern world with amazing results in both Agile and traditional environments.

Chapter 2 Action Steps

1. Review your organizational culture as compared to the ideals expressed in the Agile Manifesto. Write down the answers to the following questions:
   a. How friendly are your teams toward the idea of using Agile?
   b. How many of your teams have been trained in Agile methodologies like Scrum?
   c. How many CSMs, CSPOs and CSPs do you have in your organization?
   d. What level of buy-in do you have from the Executive-level?
      i. Note: "The number of companies planning to implement Agile development methodologies in future projects has increased from 59% in 2011 to 83% in 2012." Standish 2012 CHAOS Report
2. Would you describe your company as a collaborative environment or one that is process/tool **Driven**?
   a. Are teams punished when projects fail?
   b. Write down a strategy that will help your organization become more collaborative and less punitive.
3. How long does it take for your organization to **Deliver** a new product (i.e Working Software, etc.)?

      a. How much documentation is currently required to **Deliver** the product?

      b. What documentation is never reviewed again after the project is completed?

4. Who is the "voice of the customer" in your organization?

      a. Do you have Product Owners?

         i. If yes, are these Product Owners truly empowered to make decisions that will impact the financial outcome of the product?

      b. Do you have Product Managers?

      c. Do you have a Product Marketing team?

         i. How quickly are your projects able to respond to change?

      a. Does your organization have a formal project change management process?

      b. Which parts of the formal project change management process could be deleted or modified to help the teams respond more quickly to change?

         i. "52% of companies state that the biggest barrier to Agile adoption is the inability to change organizational culture." Standish 2012 CHAOS Report

SOME PROBLEMS WITH AGILE PROJECT IMPLEMENTATIONS

"Traditional/Waterfall projects have a success rate of 14% and Agile/Scrum projects have a success rate of 42%." Dr. Jeff Sutherland, Co-creator of Scrum

"There is just simply a lot of bad Agile going on out there." Dr. Jeff Sutherland

It is obvious from the quote above that using agile as a method for managing and running projects more than triples project success rates. However, a failure rate of 58% still represents billions of dollars of waste and loss for organizations trying to do more with less in the current difficult economic environment.

The second quote, by Dr. Sutherland, acknowledges that there is a lot of bad agile going on around the world.

We tend to agree.

But, we have found that proper, disciplined application of Business Agile principles, like the **UVF**, can accelerate success and improve profitability regardless of the type of business, NGO or nonprofit using it.

In a recent "Annual State of Agile Development Survey" by an Agile software vendor they gave the following reasons for failed Agile projects:

- 18%–None of our agile projects failed
- 12%–Company philosophy or culture at odds with core agile values
- 11%–External pressure to follow traditional waterfall processes
- 11%–A broader organizational or communications problem
- 9%–Lack of experience with agile methods
- 8%–Lack of cultural transition
- 6%–Other
- 6%–Unwillingness of team to follow agile
- 6%–Lack of management support
- 6%–Don't know
- 4%–Insufficient training
- 3%–New to agile

This vendor suggested in its report on how NOT to Fail at Agile: "When agile projects have failed, in 2/3 of these cases it was because of either failure to integrate the right people or to teach a team-based culture." The top success factors when scaling agile were as follows:

- Executive sponsorship – 23%,
- Training/workshops – 18%,
- Implementation of a common tool – 13%.

One of the main challenges for Agile is captured in the latest statistics from Scrum Alliance's own website from May of 2013:
- CSM (Certified Scrum Master)
  - ○ 221,798 certified to date
- CSPO (Certified Scrum Product Owner)
  - ○ 36,195 students to date
- CSP (Certified Scrum Professional)
  - ○ 2,718 certified to date
  - ○ of which 1,912 are active
  - ○ Including Ted and Andrew
- CSC (Certified Scrum Coach)
  - ○ 58 certified to date
  - ○ of which 54 are active
- CST (Certified Scrum Trainer)
  - ○ 148 certified to date
  - ○ of which 142 are active

The lack of qualified, experienced Agile leaders is contributing to a large number of Agile projects that fail. With only 36,195 Product Owners trained, as of May 2013, there is a huge gap in the market of available Product Owners to lead Agile projects. We assume that these certified individuals can actually function as a Product Owner in the way envisioned by Scrum. We find it interesting that sitting through a two-day training and taking a short pass/fail exam suddenly qualifies you as a Product Owner or ScrumMaster. Training is very important, but getting a "certificate" does not make a person a professional. Our observation is that, depending upon the individual's background and experience, it can take up to two years for a person to make the transformation to being truly Agile. Most companies do not factor this into their transition plans.

The people constraint becomes even more apparent if you do a quick check of simplyhired.com and search on the term "Agile." As of 22 October 2013 there are 679,616 open Agile jobs listed on the website (18 months ago a similar search produced just over 16,000 openings, so the growth curve is exploding in this area), of which:

- 4,904 **CSM** jobs
- 7,963 agile **product owner** jobs
- Of which, only 112 specifically request the **CSPO** certification
- 5,405 **CSP** jobs
- Of which only 125 are agile/**CSP**
- 686 **certified scrum coach** jobs
- 47 **certified scrum trainer** jobs

"A study conducted by Yoh based on data from CareerBuilder's Supply and Demand Portal revealed that the number of advertised agile jobs outnumbered active candidates by 4.59-to-1." That's almost a 5 to 1 ratio of Agile jobs to active candidates. The Yoh report stated that, "This skills gap has not only made it difficult for companies to quickly source quality talent on demand, but also puts them at risk of hiring technical professionals that have poor agile methodology skills."[10]

Companies understand the need to go Agile, but are probably not prepared for the fierce competition that they will face for getting the top-notch Agile talent that they will need.

Chapter 3 Action Steps

Find and write down the answers to the following questions for your organization:

1. What is your organization's current project success rate?
   a. Does anyone actually know?
   b. For Waterfall projects?
   c. For Agile projects?
   d. For Blended Projects?
2. What do you think the primary causes are for the successful projects?
   a. For the failed projects?
3. Does your organization have an HR plan and strategy to attract competent Agile talent?
   a. If not, why not?
4. Does your organization have a formal plan for obtaining Project Management certifications/credentials for your project team members?

a. What certifications/credentials is your organization going to support?
   i. PMP?
   ii. CSM, CSPO and CSP?
   iii. Six Sigma Black belt?
   iv. Etc?
5. What is the "people" organizational change management strategy for your organization?
   a. If you don't have one, then write down what it should it be.

SECTION 2 –
THE ELEMENTS OF SUCCESSFUL AGILE

CHAPTER 4

UNIFIED VISION FRAMEWORK

"For without a vision the people are unre-strained." Ancient Proverb

"The function of leadership – the number-one responsibility of a leader – is to catalyze a clear and shared vision for the organization and to secure commitment to and vigorous pursuit of that vision. This is a universal requirement of leadership."[11] Jim Collins

"Good business leaders create a vision, artic-ulate the vision, passionately own the vision, and relentlessly drive it to completion."[12] Jack Welch

I f you are not governed by **Vision**, then you will be tossed about on the stormy waters of circumstance. For most businesses, the color of the ocean doesn't matter if you're in the middle of a hurricane.

In 1992 and 1993 we (the authors) had independently arrived at the same conclusion as Jim Collins stated in the quote above and described this idea in the **UVF** that **Vision** is the key **Driver** for everything that happens in a business.

For the Executive, Senior Management, Management and Team levels a clearly **Defined Vision** needs to cascade to every level of a company. Each level then needs to link its own **Vision** back to the level above it and to the overall **Vision** of the Enterprise.

It is not enough to have a **Vision** statement. An adaptation of a Japanese proverb captures this rather well, "vision without implementation is mere fantasy. Unfocused activity without vision is truly a nightmare."

Vision-Driven

Every level in the organization needs to **Distill Agreement** and gain buy-in with its stakeholders. Having clearly **Defined Purpose, Mission** and **Vision** statements and **Distilled Agreement** with the stakeholders exponentially enhances the ability to **Deliver** the **Vision** and to do it more quickly.

This has been seen occasionally in the literature related to Project management, for example Dale Christenson and Derek Walker stated, "while the Project management literature appears to be dominated by the importance of techniques used to manage Projects, there is a noticeable gap in the literature relating to the impact of Project leadership and the development of a **Project Vision** that unites Project teams and supply chain partners as a critical success factor for Projects."[13] In the same Journal Dr. Les Labuschague and Carl Marnewick in their 2006 paper *A Structured Approach to Derive Projects from the Organizational Vision* make a similar observation on how **Vision** should instruct how Projects are selected, managed and reported. However, it is by no means the norm. For example, you will not find **Vision** mentioned in *A Guide to the Project Management Body of knowledge (PMBOK Guide) 4th Edition* and this is the ISO and ANSI Standard for Project management world-wide.

Published in 2013, The PMBOK 5th Edition mentions **Vision** 9 times (with four repeats in the Appendix's). But there is no mention in the Glossary or the Index. PMI is getting closer to a **Vision Driven**, value-based model for project management but we believe they still have a way to go before the links between Executive level Purpose, Mission, **Vision** and Strategic Initiatives cascade easily down to the task level **Delivery** points. A model like the **UVF** will help them get there.

Project management for most of its professional life has been relegated to the land of detail driving efficiency. There has been more chatter in recent years about how Project, Program and Portfolio management is becoming more of a strategic part of the enterprise structure. If this transition from operational to strategic is to occur, and we agree that it should, then we need to organize and communicate through the lens of **Vision** because that is how strategic people organize and think.

Peter Drucker once stated, "Efficiency is doing the thing right, but effectiveness is doing the right thing."[14] If all we are doing is effectively driving details without linking our activities to the over-arching **Vision** of the company then we remain operational and not strategic. In a perfect world Executives want every division, every functional area, every Project and every person making decisions at their level of authority based on the 'right thing.' They want efficiency but efficiently doing the wrong thing is still the wrong thing. The degree to which project managers and Scrum Masters succeed at **Delivering** and communicating this story is the degree to which they will be allowed to sit at the strategy table.

We recently heard of an excellent example of this successful transition of a PMO to the strategic level in West Michigan. Gordon Food Service, a privately held 10.3 billion dollar company in Grand Rapids run by the Gordon family, added a Chief Strategy Officer to their Executive Team structure. The PMO (Program Management Office) reports directly to the CSO. Perfect.

Your company may not have a CSO and may not realize the importance of **Vision** at the Project, Program and Portfolio level but that does not prevent you from organizing a PMO and individual Projects based upon this understanding. The more effectively you accomplish this linkage the more you and your PMO will be considered a strategic partner within the company.

Define Vision

Ultimately, all organizational life and function revolves around **Definitions**. What is our Purpose? What is our Mission and **Vision**? What are the strategies and goals that we are pursuing to accomplish these ends? Without a clear **Definition** there is no focus. It is like the old joke where the man mounted his horse and rode off in all directions or the ancient maxim that every man does what is right in his own eyes. Or, as Benjamin J. Parker from the article *"Strong Vision Creates Strong Project Teams"* in PM Network Magazine July 2000 observed, "a Project team without **Vision** will quickly degrade to a random grouping of people attending the same conference calls."

Kent Crawford states in Chapter One of *"An Inside Look at High Performing PMO's"* that there are three central formation themes that are found in the applications of PMO of the Year Finalists for PMI:

1. **Use a Standard Language**. This can mean something as simple as a shared lexicon for working on Projects (in which terms like "plan," "schedule," and "requirement") have been precisely **Defined**. At the other end of the scale, it can mean a methodology or multiple methodologies that connect industry

best practices with Project management standards.

2. **Educate Broadly, then Deeply**. Smart PMO leaders train widely: giving support staff and line managers and executives the basics of Project management to build supportive organization around the PMO, then focusing training on the Project managers and staff to bring their practice in line with the requirements of the organization.

3. **Collect Data Rigorously**. Most, if not all, PMO leaders today realize that the value of the PMO must be quantified.

We believe these themes do indeed reflect why a PMO would be successful and we would add that the methodology mentioned in bullet number one for us is the **UVF**. The degree to which we succeed in obtaining clear **Definitions** and **Distilled Agreements** between all Project stakeholders on the Purpose/Mission/**Vision** of the Project and the **Definition** of success is the degree we are able to measure and prove benefit realization at the end of the day. In other words, if #1 is done poorly then #2 is difficult and #3 does not matter. Whereas, if #1 is done well then #2 and #3 can follow naturally and will be accepted and agreed to by all parties. We use the language of **Vision** to establish agreement, manage change and ultimately prove and communicate value.

The core **Driver** for us in working on any Project or Program, particularly at the Enterprise level, is the language used to describe what we are doing and what we are trying to accomplish. Clarity of language is hard, continuous work and it is the platform for all success. If you cannot describe what you are doing and trying to accomplish in simple language that everyone gets and agrees to then you are severely reducing your odds of achieving your goals. Dr. Frank Luntz in his book *Words that Work* says it this way, "For words to have real impact, the public, at an absolute minimum, has to know what they mean – and how to say them and repeat them. If they don't, or can't, it is hardly a recipe for success."[15] We find this is even truer when finding the language needed to construct and communicate effectively as a Project or Program leader or in creating an Enterprise PMO regardless of methodology.

That being said, we need to give you some of our **Definitions** so that we can communicate clearly through the balance of this book.

Culture of Vision

Culture is the most difficult part for an organization to create and/or copy. A company that understands the need to change and chooses to go Agile will already be five to seven years behind in the game. For example, if one company has a 36 month cycle to bring a new product to market and one of their competitors can do the same in 12 months, by the time the first company gets to a 12 month cycle, the competitor will be now at 6 months or even 3.

Those who do not come from a Judeo-Christian background may find the verse structure (that we share from Nehemiah later in this book) is a new construct on which to reflect. To Nehemiah the scriptures were practical, sound wisdom and he aligned his life to them. So well, in fact, that the king valued his character, managerial skills and results.

Your higher **Vision** might not be the same as Nehemiah's, but it must be real, compelling and true if people are going to be drawn to it and work to accomplish it.

A core part the **UVF** is the **VSPT** model. The original **VSPT** as taught by the United States Military Academy at West Point is Vision → Strategy → Projects → Tactics. Our modified version of the **VSPT** Model is as follows:

Vision
Strategy
People
Tasks

We use "People" interchangeably with Projects, etc., since people are the ones that organize all organizational tasks into products, processes, projects, programs and portfolios (so use whichever "P" is best for your organizational context).

The theory is that: People and Tasks are linked to the organization's **Vision** and Strategies.

But, the reality is that there is usually a huge disconnect between these in every organization and that is why we put a line separating the **VS** from the **PT** above. **Vision**, as **Defined** above (including Purpose, Core Values and Attitudes, Mission and Goals) includes "**culture**" (more on that in the Figure below). In order for **VSPT** to function properly in any organization you have to have the right culture backing it up. This is crucial since it is a well known fact that culture eats portfolios, products, services, programs, projects and processes for breakfast, lunch AND dinner!

As we shared in the **4D Model** Figure at the beginning of this chapter, **VSPT** is a key component in the **4D Model's Definition** process. As a project manager or product owner, you need to **Define** the "**VSPT**" for your project and/or product, right up-front, if you want to have any hope of succeeding with your program, product, project, etc.

The competitor that is ahead in the game has the luxury of being proactive in their process improvements. The company that is behind will most likely be in a reactive mode. But, being reactive will most likely lead to the demise of the company in today's environment. The company that is behind needs to become pre-active. That is, they need to create a **Vision** that will, in the next 3 to 5 years, position themselves ahead of where their competition will be. How do you do that? Daniel Burrus, in his book *Flash Foresight* had the following Seven Flash Foresight Triggers:

- "Start with Certainty – use hard trends to see what's coming
- Anticipate – base your strategies on what you know about the future
- Transform – use technology driven change to your advantage
- Take your biggest problem and skip it – it's not the real problem anyway
- Go Opposite – look where no one else is looking to see what no one else is seeing and do what no one else is doing
- Redefine and reinvent – identify and leverage your uniqueness in powerful ways
- Direct your future – or someone else will direct it for you"[16]

If your organization exists in a reactive market situation it would be a valuable exercise to envision where you need to be in five years and aim your **Vision** toward that outcome. Burrus' book will be helpful to you in initiating that journey.

When we use the word "**Vision**" we actually are talking about a ***culture of Vision***. This includes all of the following **Definitions** for Purpose, Mission and **Vision** combined with Core Values and Beliefs working in concert to give life and direction to an organization:

- **Vision** Statement — this states what we want to be
- Mission Statement — this describes the business we are in
- Purpose Statement — this explains why we exist
- Core Values & Attitudes — who we are and what we passionately believe
- Goals and Objectives — These break the Strategies down into specific, measurable items that can be near term or long term in nature

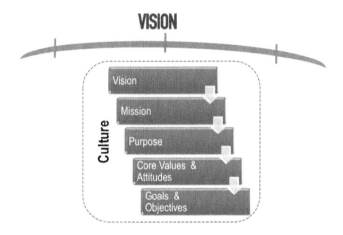

All of these items (from **Vision** on down to Goals and Objectives) that we include in "culture" work together to create, shape and form the culture of the organization. If the culture doesn't change, then the organization cannot change.

Cascading Vision

We have used a cascading structure to construct and manage Projects and PMO organizations for decades and we began talking about **Vision** being the compilation of all the underlying parts in 2000.

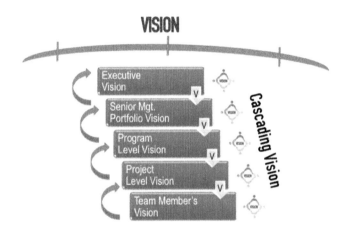

Max DePree, in his book *Leadership Jazz* said, "The goals of the organization are best met when the goals of the people in the organization are met at the same time."[17]

The technique we use to maintain the unity of **Vision** throughout the organization is cascading the **Vision** and **VSPT** at every level of the organization (and then make sure it's linked back to the previous levels in the organization).

We do this with a series of strategic planning meetings where we take the **Vision** of the organization (almost every organization we work with has a Mission statement or a **Vision** statement that can be used as a starting point) and then work with each functional area or Division to create their own specific Purpose, Mission and **Vision** statements that aim at the over-arching goals of the entire organization but are specific to their team or area. We then show the company how to construct a Purpose, Mission and **Vision** Statement for each Project and ultimately how to encourage these statements at an individual level.

By following this process you gain alignment, or unity, from the individuals performing tasks to the re-prioritization of strategic initiatives by the Executive team and it is clear up and down the organizational chart how it all fits together.

An example of how this can function effectively is the work we did with Bethany Christian Services, the largest adoption agency in the world with 1,500 employees in 90 locations. Bethany's **Vision** Statement states "We envision a world where every child is in a loving home." As we worked with the various functional teams within Bethany to create cascading Purpose, Mission and **Vision** statements the Development Team result truly stands out. In the Non-Profit world the Development group is the fund-raising team. Thus, you would think that the mission, or business that they are in, would be related to raising money to fuel the organization needs and goals. The Mission statement created by the team stated; "Connecting Resources to

Vulnerable Children." Succinct, elegant and right on the mark for what they are trying to do as a team.

The **Vision** statement, what they want to be, was equally good; "*To Model and Inspire Exceptional Giving*." As a team they felt that they needed to be models of the type of giving they were asking donors to participate in. This in turn would generate results because their work effort would spring from the reality they are living and modeling. We trust you see how this allows the functional area to live the **Organizational Vision** within the context of what they are tasked to **Deliver** in their function.

Thus, a cascading **Vision** that is different from the main **Vision** feeds the 'why' of the functional areas with the core meaning of the **True Vision** of the Enterprise.

We then create a Purpose, Mission and **Vision** statement for each Project. It has to capture in a short phrase how this Project will fulfill the Purpose, Mission and **Vision** of the team and the functional area and the entire company. All of the **Vision** statements are listed in the Project Charter and the Project Mission and **Vision** Statements are in the header for all Project documents so that the team is continually reminded 'why' they are **Delivering** on the tasks they are working on. As Max DePree said, "All of the visions, all of the strategies, all of the implementation, all of the day-to-day operations, are carried out by one potential water carrier or another, always working in concert with, or in need of, another water carrier." At Herman Miller a water carrier is the person **Delivering** on a task. We need our water carriers to understand, believe and own the **Vision** to such a deep degree that their decisions reflect and contribute to it.

To again quote Dr. Luntz (pg 70), "While the study of the impact of language may be a science, the actual creation of effective communication is an art." Exactly.

Even in the art of proper **Delivery**, however, effective communication is affected by how closely our **Vision** talk lines up with our **Vision** walk.

The Four Visions

There are four types of **Vision** that exist in any organization. And they all need to be understood and dealt with properly to arrive at true **Vision**. The four types are:

1. **True Vision**
2. **Stated Vision**
3. **Implied Vision**
4. **Actual Vision**

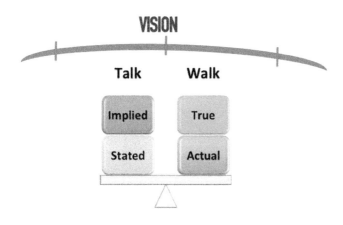

Vision is in balance when the Walk and Talk match. First, we need to understand **True Vision**. The true **Vision** is the sweet spot inside the organization on which the executive should actually be focusing. The sweet spot has many names: "competitive advantage," "hedgehog," "purple cow," "unique selling proposition," etc. **Distilling** the **Definition** of a true **Vision** can only happen over time and emerges from the pressure cooker of disagreement, where all opposing views have been aired, evaluated and the combination of the best parts of each idea creates the true **Vision**. The true **Vision** statement, once it has been **Distilled**, should then be crafted into a short phrase that is easy to remember and even easier to communicate.

Every company goes through the process of creating the **stated Vision** that they share with the world, the "official **Vision**" of the organization. The true **Vision** should shape the stated **Vision**.

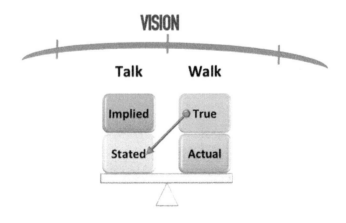

True Vision should always shape the **Stated Vision**. However, if you were to take the top executive team from your organization, put them in a room, and ask each one write the **Vision** statement from memory on a piece of blank paper and then compare the results, you would probably find as we have that there would be twelve different versions of the stated **Vision**, even if only ten people were in the room. Why is that? Because almost without exception the stated **Vision** is too long, generic and doesn't reflect the true **Vision**.

When we work with Executive Teams to help clarify the Purpose, Mission and **Vision** of the organization we always begin with this exercise. We give them sixty seconds to write out, from memory, the Purpose, Mission and **Vision** statements for the company. We have done this exercise with over fifty companies in the past and so far only one group has succeeded in knowing their statements, more-or-less, word for word.

We believe that not having internalized the organization's **Vision** is key reason why 58% of Agile projects and 86% of traditional projects fail. The stated **Vision** may be printed on slick glossy paper, but that doesn't make it true.

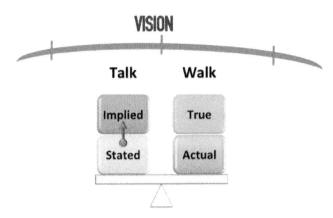

Stated Vision in action is the **Implied Vision**. It is because there is another dynamic at work as well and it's called implied **Vision**. The implied **Vision** is the reflection of each leader's walk. If a leader's walk and talk match, then the implied and actual **Visions** will converge with and match the true **Vision** for the organization:

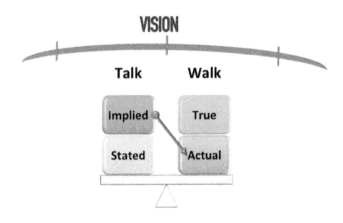

Implied Vision should align with the **Actual Vision**. But, in most organizations, this is where the walk and the talk diverge from what's printed in the marketing brochures and reality. An example would be if we state "quality is job 1" and yet our product never has the best quality record, and the people in the organization never see any leadership support for increased quality, then the stated **Vision** is not reality.

Everybody sees the disconnect and the result is that if you have good people, they will try to figure out, as best they can, what the true **Vision** is and align themselves to that **Vision**. If the stated **Vision** and the implied **Vision** do not line up what do you have? An **actual Vision** that is **fractured**:

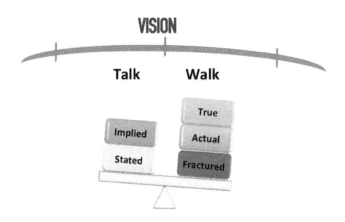

If the **Implied Vision** doesn't align with the **Actual Vision**, then it is fractured. Allowing broken implied **Vision(s)** at the leadership level to go unchecked produces a **Fractured Vision** for the company that is out of balance and splintered. When the actual **Vision** is created by organizational dissonance and division (i.e. "division" means two **Visions**) we find that 'every person does what is right in his or her own eyes' becomes the norm. You have as many **Visions** as you have people. And this may or may not line up with what is best for the organization. More often than not it becomes the ego of the leaders that determines what is prioritized and the team ends up having to resort to personal heroics to save the day. Others resort to defensive (*"CYA"*) task management in order to mitigate the effect that the fractured **Vision** has on them. An example of this is when you have put your and your team's full effort to comply with and **Deliver** according to the stated **Vision**, but then you end up being punished by the organization for doing what you thought was the right thing. This is unjust behavior and the team and the leadership knows it. This demotivates future endeavors and kills innovation. Max DePree is accurate in his assessment when he states, "Unjust leaders paralyze their followers."[18]

Paralyzed and still trying to do the right thing but the activity which they assumed lined up with the stated **Vision** did not line up with someone else's actual **Vision** or ego. A fractured **Vision** might be the result of some undeclared tribal war or just an unexplained "that's the bottom line" but the result is the same; trust is broken and full effort dies.

Whatever a team has determined the organization's true **Vision** to be is what they will use as their actual **Vision** and this will shape their decision-making and change management choices negatively and cripple what may be an otherwise excellent team. It is the consequence of their best guess of what the true **Vision** should be and expending the effort to re-align with the new understanding.

Jim Collins explains the dynamic this way; "The most important element of leadership effectiveness is authentically living the **Vision** of the company. The values and ambitions of a company are not instilled entirely by what leaders say; they're instilled primarily by what leaders do. In a healthy company, there are no inconsistencies between what is said and what is believed deep down – the values come from within the leaders and imprint themselves on the organization through day-to-day activity."[19] When inconsistencies are exposed, people adapt and try to figure out what the true **Vision** is. Inconsistency is death. The result is cultural chaos. The cultural impact of this chaos is that everything slows down. If you have not been paying attention up to this point we believe that with the speed at which the world is changing we cannot afford to be slow.

Then, just to keep things interesting, every six to twelve months companies roll out new strategic initiatives or reorganizations. Sometimes, they even roll out a new **Vision** statement. Over time the strategies migrate into something that has little, or nothing, to do with the original stated **Vision** of the company. This creates organizational **Vision** fatigue and the leaders just can't seem to understand why people deliberately choose to ignore their directives. Sometimes companies will even bring in a new leader from outside the organization in order to try to shake things up and break the resistance to the behavioral changes that are needed to renew the culture. According to the research conducted in "Good to Great," bringing in an "outside change agent was negatively correlated with a sustained transformation from good to great."[20] This could be due to the first line of management that reports directly to the new leader end up circling the wagons and present a united front that neutralizes the leader's ability to create the positive change that was desired. These company "antibodies" are the dark side of a unified **Vision**.

When this happens, a leader may be tempted to make the mistake of invoking the power of their position to effect change rather than using personal authority to lead. For example, a leader can use the power of the position and demand a 20% across-the-board cut in all Projects that are in the pipeline without realizing that some of the most critical Projects (necessary for the survival of the organization) could end up being killed because they weren't linked to the true **Vision**. If you don't know what the true **Vision** is, then Projects that are linked to the true **Vision** can be cut for personal or political reasons. We call this the "*unencumbered by knowledge, we acted...*" phenomena.

The use of power to motivate tends to slide down the slippery slope toward the Theory X style management that uses fear and intimidation as a motivator. And while it may never be actually stated by the people being led, the more that power is used to demand change, the more fear rises as the true motivator. Studies have shown that fear as a motivational tool is only useful in short time frames and crises situations. Long-term use of fear as a motivator destroys innovation and effectiveness. It bogs down the speed at which the organization can react and adapt to changing market conditions.

Dwight Eisenhower once said, "It is always easier to pull a string than to push it." This is what we mean by leading from personal authority. Whether it's by serving, which is the **Definition** of a Level 5 leader in "Good to Great,"[21] or by demonstrating with words and actions your alignment with the true **Vision**, leadership from authority always achieves the best results. Authority energizes the intangible assets inherent inside every organization. These exist in the white space of the organizational chart. When a leader pulls the intangibles together by means of a cohesive, true **Vision** that is lived by the entire team, then exponential results are the natural outcome.

Still, a charismatic leader can have a clear understanding of the company's true **Vision**, lead from authority and fail to achieve the desired results. How can that happen? By assuming agreement. It is essential for each and every person to buy-in to his or her part of the true **Vision**. Leaders understand that the first step to gaining agreement with any team is to have clear **Definitions** upon which everyone agrees. When the **Definitions** are in continual flux, it becomes difficult for team members to focus. This is why clear Purpose, Mission and **Vision** statements are needed at the function and Project level. When the **Definitions** are clear-cut and agreement has been reached, then **Distilling** the tasks into a cohesive result becomes almost effortless and fast adaptation to changing conditions becomes easier and less stressful.

If power is used to force agreement, then the person performing the tasks has no option other than to complete the task as **Defined** by the boss. Creativity is killed. Team members no longer come up with creative solutions to execute the tasks quicker, with less effort and with greater impact. Conversely, if personal authority is used to gain agreement and thus inspire the completion of the tasks, then people begin to recognize that the leader is there to support them in achieving success for the entire team. Options are examined and inspired solutions are revealed.

Thus far we've identified three mortal leadership sins (i.e. not walking the talk, leading from power and not authority and assuming agreement) that can derail even the most adept and agile of leaders. Understanding these root causes is a great place to start, and frankly they have to be addressed and dealt with in order to obtain and maintain organization strength and excellence. In the process of addressing these core organizational challenges a leader can indeed control and accelerate the Project portfolio. If you have a model or framework that is short, memorable, and remarkable and that is linked to the true **Vision**, then it can become an effective tool for prioritizing Projects as well as managing them and the enterprise.

The reason a simple model or framework is most effective is because of the natural dynamic of change. It doesn't matter what your Project structure is today, you can be certain that tomorrow the market's going to change, the customer is going to change, resources are going to change, financial components are going to change and leadership is going to change. If you have a clear, true **Vision**, and this is reflected and articulated throughout the company down to the task level then any changes that occur at the any level can be quickly aligned back to the true **Vision**. Conversely, if your **Vision** is ill **Defined**, not memorable and unwieldy, then the Projects in your portfolio will certainly still change, most likely in a negative or unproductive way, as people try to guess how the change fits the actual **Vision**.

But, alignment becomes unlikely.

That's unfortunate since it's as simple as walking the talk and not just talking the talk. Talk is cheap. If your actions speak so loud that your team can't hear what you are saying, then it's time to take a step back and look in the mirror.

Make sure you take the time to identify what the true **Vision** is.

Articulate what that **Vision** is for each of your functional areas, the Portfolios, Programs and Projects and then lead by example. Do the work. Do your homework. Spend more effort with **Definitions** and **Distill Agreements** that link to the true **Vision**. Use the true **Vision** as a tool to manage and lead all Project efforts and the creativity needed within the Project teams will rise and amazing results will occur. Using the **UVF**, or any other **Vision** clarifying model, and applying it correctly will create a truly **Vision** focused culture where good people are free to create outstanding value.

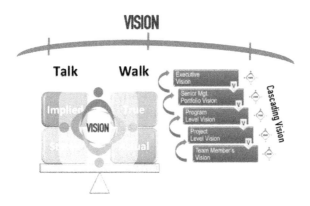

When **Vision** is in Balance, Cascading it through the Organization becomes Natural. All of the above discussion falls apart if the leaders or the team members do not believe that the **Vision** is true or that it is true for them. The nuclear fuel of a clearly **Defined Vision** is belief. The team must believe in the **Vision** and its ultimate success for **Vision** to work. They won't believe it if you don't own it, believe it and demonstrate it with your walk.

Ultimately it comes down to leadership and as we quoted above, Jack Welch, summed it up this way, "Good business leaders create a vision, articulate the vision, passionately own the vision, and relentlessly drive it to completion."[22]

Why Simple is Better

Why is this important? An old Greek proverb states that "A fish stinks from the head down" or in other words if the leaders do not get it then the troops will not get it.

We have found over the years that for a statement to be memorable and communicable within an organization it cannot be longer that seven to nine words. Our preference is five to seven. Let's demonstrate this. Here are two statements we drew from a couple of company websites:

1. *"Our mission is to satisfy the needs of our customers through wholesale distribution. We strive to be, and to be viewed as, the highest value provider of such products and services in the market in which we choose to compete. The major resource behind our success will be our high-performance team of associates who will share in the financial benefits of this success."*

2. *"The mission of the company is to:*
   - *Promote the best interests of the company and act as an advocate in company issues.*
   - *Promote and protect the integrity of the company plan.*
   - *Ensure that the business opportunity today is as good or better for future generations.*
   - *Act as an advisory group to the parent company."*

Now, turn this page over and try to remember any part of the mission statements that you just read above. Unless you are blessed with a photographic memory, then you probably caught a few words and the rest is off in the mist and gone.

Next, let's look at Nokia's Mission statement (remember, mission is the business you are in):

- *Connecting People*

Now turn the page over again and try to remember what you just read.

The vast majority of you turned over the page and said "Connecting People" because it is short and memorable. It clearly articulates a mission that can change and adapt as the market morphs because it is not tied to a specific technology or device. If Nokia had stayed myopically tied to its original mission it would still be in the lumber business but its mission statement today is highly effective and communicates within and without the company what they are trying to do.

Short and accurate is always best. It can be hard work getting to that point but it is necessary effort whether you intend to move a Project or change an organization. However, just because it is brief does not mean it is clear. Do not stop until you have language that is both terse and clearly communicates. We need this because as humans we tend to forget and many times what we remember is wrong.

"A mind is a terrible thing to waste" has been the slogan for the United Negro College Fund for many years. We would like to take this phrase and twist it a bit for effect and to make our point regarding the need for continuous reminders. In this case it should read "a mind is a terrible thing to trust". What do we mean? Rudolph Flesch, in his book *The Art of Clear Thinking,* talks about how ineffective and errant our memory is, even immediately after observing the event or reading an article. Our minds tend to 'fill in' details that did not exist to map the data to our beliefs.[23] This is a true dynamic that must be considered in all human communication; things are not as clear as we think. We need to remind ourselves often 'why are we here and why does it matter' or other competing ideas and priorities rise up and take over.

If this is true, and we believe that it is, then why all the worry about **Definitions**? This is precisely the point. If our starting point is unclear communication then extra effort and ongoing effort is required to create and maintain organizational unity. It is not automatic and can never be assumed.

Start Where You are At

"You can't build a reputation on what you're going to do," was a very wise observation from Henry Ford. You may be reading this book and thinking "these are great ideas," but not acting on them would be unfortunate. We have heard back from people we have trained that they took the framework back into their work environment (from Project to Enterprise level) and began to see organizational results the very next day. It does require that you act. Start. You do not have to try to boil the ocean.

Look at the realm you live in and determine where to start.

Create a **VSPT** at the level you own (Vision, Strategy, People and Tasks is further elaborated in our White Paper on Unified Vision/Enterprise Agile that can be found on our website, www.pmobrothers.com, as well as in this book), work on clarifying the **Definitions** within your current company. **Distill Agreement** by linking it to the Enterprise **Vision** and once you succeed migrate that success to the next Project or Program.

If you are leading a Project then take the Enterprise **Vision** and mission statements and place them at the top of your next Project Charter. Then, before you do anything else, craft a Purpose, Mission and **Vision** statement for the Project. It is best to create this with your team but at a minimum create one and then show the team and work with it until you have agreement that "yes, this describes the **Project Vision** and we agree this is what we are going to do." Add the statements to the artifacts you use to manage the Project and refer to them often, particularly when a change occurs. We require any change to go back through the Four D's of the framework to make sure that the change does not alter our **Definitions** or **Distilled Agreements** and that all appropriate stakeholders agree with that assessment (or the approved alterations to the plan). This maintains unity within the team and toward the **Vision** of the Enterprise, functional area and Project.

If you have responsibility for developing or running a Company, Program Management Office (PMO) or Project, then use the **UVF** to organize and manage the flow of this effort. It will give you the tools needed to communicate at the strategic level and to manage the various teams down to the task level.

Finally, one of the most important reasons you need a clear understanding of the organizational **Vision** and how it applies at the Portfolio, Program, Project and task level deliverables is the effect it has on decision-making. If Project Management is to be viewed as a strategic addition to an Executive Team's tool kit then it must communicate in the language of that Team. Executive language will always revolve around **Vision**. A properly functioning PMO will thus construct its own Purpose, Mission and **Vision** statements that align with the company Purpose, Mission and **Vision**. We call this a "**Cascading Vision**" and that **Vision** should inform decisions down to the smallest task allowing our work to be effective in addition to efficient. When communicating why choice 'A' was picked over choices 'B-G' it should be described through the prism of that **Vision**. This allows continuous alignment and maintenance of unity, freeing people to make good decisions based on the clear **Vision**.

The results speak for themselves.

Chapter 4 Action Steps

Find and write down the answers to the following questions for your organization:

1. Does your organization have a **Vision**, Mission and/or Purpose statement?
   a. If so, write it down.
   b. If not, write the **Vision** as you would understand it.
      i. Then ask your CEO if he/she agrees.

2. What is the **Vision** for your Product?
   a. If you don't have one, write the **Product Vision** as you would understand it.
      i. Then ask your Product Owner/ Sponsor if he/she agrees.
   b. How does that **Product Vision** link back to the overall **Vision**?

3. What is the **Vision(s)** for the Project(s) that will be part of creating your Product?
   a. If you don't have one, write the **Project Vision** as you would understand it.
      i. Then ask your PMO/Project Sponsor if he/she agrees.
   b. How does that **Project Vision** link back to the overall **Vision**?
   c. Do you personally agree with the above stated **Visions**?
      i. How do you articulate this to your team and Stakeholders?

SECTION 3 – NEHEMIAH'S SUCCESS USING AGILE PRINCIPLES

In this section we are going to follow Nehemiah's journey and the Agile principles that he applied to his project.

―――――

CHAPTER 5

THE BACK STORY
FOR NEHEMIAH'S PROJECT

"It must be remembered that there is nothing more difficult to plan, more doubtful of success, nor more dangerous to manage than the creation of a new system. For the initiator has the enmity of all who would profit by the preservation of the old institutions and merely lukewarm defenders in those who would gain by the new ones."
Nicholi Machiavelli in The Prince 1513 A.D.

To get a better understanding of the environment in which Nehemiah was working, we first need to take a look at the historical context. Originally, the project Nehemiah was proposing was a failed project that had been halted by a stop work order issued by a previous king. An executive order was required to change the status of this project and Nehemiah knew it.

Nehemiah was a senior leader in service to the king (the cupbearer to the king was an officer of high rank given to only a few, trusted individuals throughout history). The king's cupbearer in an organization of this size would have likely have had hundreds of people reporting to him and would have had sufficient budgets with which to work to carry out the king's orders. And each major festival and/or event was a project that would have required management, stewardship and oversight by the cupbearer.

But, before Nehemiah there was Ezra and Esther. They paved the way for Nehemiah's part of the project which in some respects could be considered phase two in the restarted project to restore Jerusalem:

1. Phase 1: The final renovation of and improvements for the interior and exterior features of the Temple under Ezra's direction.
2. Phase 2: Rebuilding the Walls and restoring the gates under the leadership of Nehemiah.

Ezra was still there in Jerusalem when Nehemiah rebuilt the walls and in Nehemiah 8 Ezra read the law out loud to all the people after the walls were finished.

The road map for the projects that Ezra and Nehemiah led looked like this:

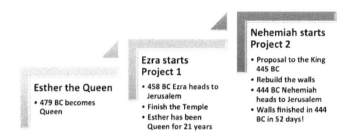

Esther the Queen
- 479 BC becomes Queen

Ezra starts Project 1
- 458 BC Ezra heads to Jerusalem
- Finish the Temple
- Esther has been Queen for 21 years

Nehemiah starts Project 2
- Proposal to the King 445 BC
- Rebuild the walls
- 444 BC Nehemiah heads to Jerusalem
- Walls finished in 444 BC in 52 days!

Esther became Queen in 479 BC. Esther was a Jew. And her story was about how the Jewish people avoided extermination at the hands of Haman who tricked the king into issuing a decree that all Jews would be killed in one day. It's interesting that even the king was not able to retract his original decree due the the way their laws were set-up. Once the king's seal was on the scroll, it could not be rescinded. So, instead he came up with a creative solution and issued a new decree that the Jews would have the right to defend themselves against anyone trying to kill them. That was genius on the part of the king and demonstrated brilliant leadership. Haman had inteneded to hang Mordecai (Esther's uncle) and his family on the gallows that he had built. The king had Haman hanged on those gallows instead. It is not wise to trick the king or to use the law of the land against him.

In the years that followed, up until 458 BC, when Ezra began his project, obviously Queen Esther and her uncle Mordecai (a Jew that had been given the number 1 administrative position in the kingdom) exerted influence on the king. This positioned both

Ezra, and subsequently Nehemiah, favorably in the king's eyes to restart and complete this project.

In 445 BC when Nehemiah went before king Artaxerxes with his "phase 2" project proposal, the king was already predisposed to approve this request. The king had already invested over $3 million of his own money in Ezra's project 13 years prior to finish up the final touches to the Temple in Jerusalem.

Any executive who has invested significantly and has close associates with a vested interest in the project is more likely to be sympathetic toward a successor project (i.e. phase 2). Clearly, executive buy-in was not an issue for Nehemiah. However, if your project does not align to your organization's Purpose, Mission and **Vision**, and does not have clear executive buy-in, you will very likely experience problems.

Even with that pre-existing favor, Nehemiah was still "very afraid." If you went in front of the king and you were sad, that was grounds for immediate execution. His request was to overturn the previous decree of king Cyrus that the walls of Jerusalem not be rebuilt.

His project request required a change in the law that could only be done by a new edict from the new king. If the king disagreed, then Nehemiah risked the death penalty. Very few project managers, ScrumMasters or Product Owners in today's environment risk death if their project proposal is not accepted. I suspect project leaders or stakeholders would probably be more careful with the projects they propose if death were on the line. Death brings a certain clarity to decision making.

Executives today are increasingly espousing "Agile" and Agile thinking as a means to be more productive, profitable and to bring product and services to the market more quickly. However, the personal transition required to permit their organization to become truly Agile can be a long, disruptive and grueling journey. A project to transition an organization from a traditional, command-and-control culture to an Agile ethos, requires significant transformation. A complete change of this magnitude can take up to seven years, or more, although positive benefits can be realized as early as 90 to 120 days into the transition.

One of the most important things for an Executive to do when embarking on this level of change is to **Define** and **Distill** a clear **Vision** for the transformation of the organization to Agile.

Nehemiah and Vision

In looking for a case study to describe what we've intuitively been doing for the last two decades with the **UVF**, a business agile leadership methodology, we came across the most incredible **Agile project** of all-time, **completed in only 52 days** ... almost 2,500 years before agile became a buzzword: Nehemiah's agile rebuilding of the walls of Jerusalem. And we all thought Agile was something new?

The **UVF** is a leadership and management framework that we have been using in its present form for the past decade. The roots of the framework are found in Luke 2:52...

*"And Jesus grew in **wisdom** and **stature**, and in **favor** with **God** and **men**."*

This verse is incredible wisdom for managing and leading people, projects and organizations. At the personal level we deal with the **mental, physical, social and spiritual** lives of our team members and stakeholders and this is mirrored in the above verse (wisdom → mental, stature → physical, favor with men → social; and, favor with God → spiritual or **Vision** alignment at the individual level). We illustrate this with the following simple picture:

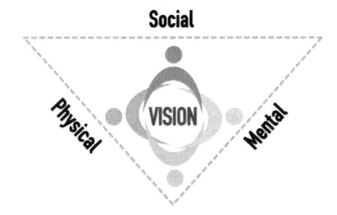

The exact same model carries over into organizational structure (mental → **business content or knowldge**, physical → **tools and technology**, social → **relationships**; and spiritual → **Vision**). When you have a team that have a **Vision** and an agreed upon set of deliverables, then you have the foundation of a successful project.

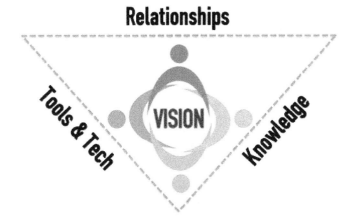

For example, we see this **principle (but used in the negative)** in Genesis 11:6 where we read:

> *"The LORD said, "If as **one people** speaking the **same language** they have begun to do this, then **nothing** they **plan** to do **will be impossible for them**."*

The 1L + 1M + 1P = 1V Formula from the verse above is one of the most simple, elegant tools you'll ever use for focusing your project team's **Vision** and linking it all together.

1L + 1M + 1P = 1V

1 Language

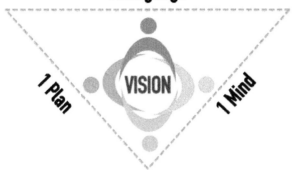

1L. It's really all about **Definitions**. Your project, organization, etc. will rise or fall depending on how well you manage your **Definitions**. Ever had a customer come to you and say, "oh by the way, can we make this one 'small' change...?" The minute that you have a change in **Definitions** is the point in time where you now have a new project.

Definitions are a key component of the 1L + 1M + 1P = 1V formula (one language + one mind + one plan = one vision). You cannot achieve **one language** if people have different **Definitions** for common terms and concepts. Everyone needs to be singing from the same page of music. This doesn't mean that everyone has to speak the same spoken language (English, Swedish, Finnish, French, etc.) ... but that everyone on the team has a common, agreed-to set of **Definitions**.

1M. If everyone is speaking the same language, then it becomes easier to create a team where everyone is of the **same mind**. However, to prevent groupthink, **Distillation** has to occur so that all ideas have been examined and agreed to by the team. Open and honest communications are key components to the 1M part of this formula. If people have hidden agendas or political motives, then the project is already at risk of failure. Having **one mind**, free from groupthink, is the target.

It's essential to capture the mind share of your team members to succeed and Nehemiah did this by linking the **Project Vision** (rebuilding the walls) to the **Personal vision** (no longer living in disgrace). **Distillation** is the key for removing politics and the negative impact that it has on successfully implementing your project, program or portfolio. That's powerful!!!

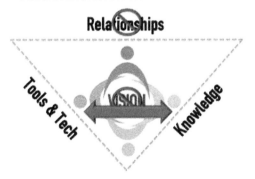

1P. Planning goes much more smoothly and quickly when you have a team that speaks the same language and that is on the same wavelength mentally. Putting together a unified plan is more efficient when the **Definitions** are agreed to and the plan is the result of real **Distillation** done by the team. The following Figure outlines some of the team roles involved in creating and **Distilling** your plan.

The 1L + 1M + 1P formula deals with the "who" dimension in a project, program or portfolio. **Vision** answers the question "why?" **Vision Driven** value should be the goal of any project and there are really only 3 reasons to do any project, program, etc. in a for-profit organization:

1. "Increase Revenues
2. Reduce costs
3. Mitigate, reduce or eliminate risk"[24]

Clearly understanding **Vision** is key for achieving 1L + 1M + 1P. We have found that it is best if a project **Vision** statement is 5 – 7 words long. It needs to be memorable and easy to communicate. **Vision** statements that are many lines or longer (i.e. paragraphs) end up being very difficult to remember or to accurately repeat. Complexity is the enemy of greatness.

Keep your **Vision** statement simple, remarkable and memorable. Nehemiah's **Vision** could have been boiled down to 5 words: rebuilt walls and rebuilt people.

Genesis 11:6 is the origin for our 1 + 1 + 1 = 1 formula (1 Language + 1 Mind + 1 Plan = 1 Vision; or, 1L + 1M + 1P = 1V) that we have used in the **UVF** for the past two decades. We have blended Luke 2:52 with Genesis 11:6 and have drawn it in the following picture with the **4D Model**:

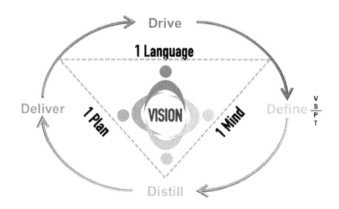

In other words **Vision = 1L + 1M + 1P**. Anywhere that you see just "**Vision**" in the middle circle of any of our images, you can automatically include 1L, 1M and 1P with "**Vision**."

In the title of our book we mentioned "projects" and not just "project." This is because the core of all Agile was already in use for the building of the Tower of Babel some 4,000+ years ago.

Want to stop a project in it's tracks?

Simply confuse the language of the team, change the **Definitions**.

The iterative **4D Model** is a key tool that is core to our leadership and management framework. The four "**D**s" are the framework for how we lead, manage and **Drive** successful teams, projects, programs and portfolios.

If one of the key things that you walk away with from reading this book is an understanding on how to apply this ancient wisdom to your projects, programs, portfolios and organizations, then you will have already, by many, many times over, multiplied the value that you bring to your work and organization.

Before we explore the Book of Nehemiah, we felt that it would be good to highlight some of the tools and techniques that Nehemiah utilized that could be classified as Agile Artifacts.

The Back Story for Nehemiah's Project

Agile Artifact(s)	How Nehemiah Used the Artifact
Clear Vision	Rebuilt walls of Jerusalem
Executive Buy-in	The King & Queen of Babylon approved and funded the project, including sending 150 Military Officers to assist Nehemiah with the leadership
Strong Product Owner with Authority	Nehemiah *(i.e. the single, wringable neck)*
Small Steering Committee	King & Queen of Babylon and Nehemiah
High-level Simple Organizational Structure	Artaxerxes (King of Babylon), Nehemiah, the Trans-Euphrates Governors, the Army Officers, the Cavalry and Asaph the King's forest keeper
ScrumMasters Facilitators	42 Team Leaders, plus over 150 Military Leaders
Team Members	49,942 (the 42 Team Leaders are included in this count)
Self-organized and self-directed teams	See Chapter 3 Verse 5 gives an example where the Team Leads refused to do the work, but the team got the work done anyway
Flat Organization	1:333 was the ratio of Leadership to Workers
Retrospective(s)	Reviewed the wall when completed to half its intended height and upon completion they celebrated the completion of the Walls. Their enemies stood back and experienced the Nehemiah Effect
Adaptation / Adjusting to Risk and Change	When the enemies tried to interfere with the project initially; and, when they failed with that, then they tried psychological warfare along with a negative public relations campaign
Product Backlog	All of the logistics, requisitions of materials, shipping, putting together the leadership team, etc. necessary for the start of the project took over a year for initiation and planning
Project lift-off / Sprint 0	Nehemiah inspects the walls (i.e. Sprint Planning) and then has the kick-off meeting with everyone to share the Vision
Daily Scrum (Stand-ups)	Held at a meal everyday: "...there were at my table one hundred and fifty Jews and officials, besides those who came to us from the nations that were around us."
Length of Sprint(s)	Approximately 26 days since they did a Sprint Review at the point in time that the walls were to half their height and they completed the project in 52 Days was definitely a Sprint
Sprint Backlog	Unknown, but daily adjustments were made to deal with external and internal risks (i.e. carrying the bricks in one hand and their spear/sword in the other)
Length of Project Implementation	52 Days

Chapter 5 Action Steps

1. Does your personal **Vision**, Mission and Purpose align with your current:
   a. Project?
   b. Product?
   c. Organization?
2. Use the Table above (a copy of the template is on our website at www.pmobrothers.com) and fill in the right column with how you plan to use the Agile Artifacts with your project.
3. Are there any sections of the table that are missing answers for your project?
   a. Write out your backlog items to fill in the missing answers.

CLEAR DEFINITIONS

Note: As we go through the following Chapters from the Book of Nehemiah (chapter by chapter) *text in italics are the actual verses* from the book of Nehemiah while normal text or **bold text** are additional commentary and other verses included by the authors.

Right up front, Nehemiah let us know that in his book he is **Delivering** the **final product/project report** to his stakeholders. Nehemiah utilized Agile techniques to succeed in his project and throughout this book we will be using Nehemiah as our case study on successful Agile project management.

Let's take a look a Nehemiah chapter 1 that includes Nehemiah's Prayer for repentance and forgiveness for himself and the entire stakeholder group (the nation of Israel).

Verse 1 answers the **who?, what?, when?** and **where?** questions every Product Owner, ScrumMaster and project manager must learn to ask:

1 The words (what – a report) of Nehemiah the son of Hacaliah (who). Now it happened in the month Chislev, in the twentieth year (when), while I was in Susa the capitol (where),

Verses 2 and 3 give us the answer to the question "**why**?" And what the situation was for the previous project that tried to repair the walls while at the same time rebuilding the Temple in Jerusalem:

2 that Hanani, one of my brothers, and some men from Judah came; and I asked them concerning the Jews who had escaped and had survived the captivity, and about Jerusalem.

It's clear that Nehemiah was concerned for his homeland and tribe and that concern prompted his questions. Part of the **Definition** (**D1**) process is **Defining** what it is that you are passionate about as we'll see below.

3 They said to me, "The remnant there in the province who survived the captivity are in great distress and reproach, and the wall of Jerusalem is broken down and its gates are burned with fire."

Nehemiah asked for and received a report of the situation in Jerusalem, a clear **Definition** of the problem. Nehemiah's starting point was a historic understanding of what had been done and attempted in Jerusalem over the past 13 years. The Temple had been rebuilt. It then began functioning again under the direction of Ezra with the approval and financial support of king Artaxerxes. The original work on the finalized rebuilding of the temple and reconstruction of the wall (Phase two of the restoration of the city) had begun under the rule of king Cyrus but was halted successfully via the influence of the local rulers of the non-Hebrew tribes by appealing to Artaxerxes (the first). It was a failed project due to political infighting. Isn't it great that we have grown so much culturally over the millennia that we never see sound projects die as a result of political infighting?

Some human realities remain the same even after thousands of years of history have passed. Ezra had successfully finished off the rebuilding of the temple but was not successful in completing the wall, which left the people who lived in Jerusalem vulnerable to assault.

In verse 3 Nehemiah is confronting the brutal facts (the walls and gates of Jerusalem had been destroyed and were in ruins) and so he clearly **Defined** (**D1**) the problem.

This is the classic "problem-solution" technique: we have a problem and here's the solution to repair the problem. It would be good to note here that every good Product Owner, ScrumMaster and project manager knows that it's not enough to be able to identify and communicate problems, but the thing the separates world-class Product Owners, ScrumMasters and project managers from the rest of the crowd is the ability to offer solutions to the problems they encounter. It's good to remind our program and port-folio managers of this from time to time as well.

Already in the first 3 verses of the book of Nehemiah, we have the answers to the who, what, when, where and why questions. The first attempt to rebuild Jerusalem had already failed and succumbed to external politics. Hardly the **Vision** of a project destined for success. Even before Nehemiah got started, he had to deal with an on-site team that was totally demoralized. How many of you would "volunteer" to run a project like that? The normal human reaction would be to cut your losses and beat a hasty retreat as quickly as possible.

But, we believe that Nehemiah understood one of the most important project management principles ever recorded in all of history (to that point in time), and it was penned by one of the wisest people to have ever walked the planet, king Solomon. He shared with us the following in Proverbs 29:

> "Where there is no vision, the people perish: but he that keepeth the law, happy is he."[25] In the NASB translation this verse reads, "Where there is no vision, the people are unrestrained, But happy is he who keeps the law."[26]

In the Swedish translation of this verse, it uses the word picture of someone who has opened the barn doors, let all of the horses out of the barn, and then the horses have all run wild and free. It's the idea of where there is no **Vision**, the people cast off restraint. Basically, if you have no **Vision**, you will die.

This applies to the personal level, the project level, the program level, the portfolio level and the division level all the way to the top of the organization.

Now, we will see in verse 4 that Nehemiah took ownership of the problem at a personal level. We are certain that you will agree that all Product Owners, ScrumMasters and project managers have worked with projects that, if possible, could have used a healthy dose of Divine help. Nehemiah was no different but he actually asked:

4 When I heard these words, I sat down and wept and mourned for days; and I was fasting and praying before the God of heaven.

Nehemiah's response to this news demonstrated his passion for the successful completion of this project. It resonated in the core of his being that this was not right and needed to be resolved. He had a higher **Vision** for the completion of this effort. At this point he could have easily echoed the response of Jake and Elmo in the movie "The Blues Brother's"that was "we are on a mission from God!" First he aligned his own heart and mind to the **Vision** and what he knew was needed for success. In Good to Great terms he had all the elements of the Hedgehog that Jim Collins says are needed for any enterprise to succeed:

1. Can you be the best in the world at this? Nehemiah believed and proved that he could **Deliver** at a world class level what was needed for the wall to be rebuilt.

2. Do you have an Economic **Driver**? The king would hopefully be backing the project to the full.
3. And Do you have a Passion for the work?

These verses demonstrate the depth of Nehemiah's passion to see Jerusalem's wall repaired and restored. The Hedgehog was fully in place for this project. Jim Collins would be proud.

The most important **Definition** (**D1**) for your project is the **Vision**. The second most important **Definition** (**D1**) is how your project's **Vision** links back to the **Vision** of your organization. It must be clear, succinct and understood by all.

5 I said, "I beseech You, O Lord God of heaven, the great and awesome God, who preserves the covenant and lovingkindness for those who love Him and keep His commandments, 6 let Your ear now be attentive and Your eyes open to hear the prayer of Your servant which I am praying before You now, day and night, on behalf of the sons of Israel Your servants, confessing the sins of the sons of Israel which we have sinned against You; I and my father's house have sinned. 7 We have acted very corruptly against You and have not kept the commandments, nor the statutes, nor the ordinances which You commanded Your servant Moses. 8 Remember the word which You commanded Your servant Moses, saying, 'If you are unfaithful I will scatter you among the peoples; 9 but if you return to Me and keep My commandments and do them, though those of you who have been scattered were in the most remote part of the heavens, I will gather them from there and will bring them to the place where I have chosen to cause My name to dwell.' 10 They are Your servants and Your people whom You redeemed by Your great power and by Your strong hand.

Here Nehemiah had gone through a root cause analysis and determined the corrective action needed to bring success where others had failed. There were internal **Vision** issues that had to be resolved.

The most important **Definition** for your project is the **Vision** for your project and how your project's **Vision** links to the **Vision** of your organization. But, it's the second half of verse 5 that we're going to focus on at this point in Nehemiah, because in verse five Nehemiah almost quotes, verbatim, the second part of Proverbs 29, when he said:

"...who preserves the covenant and lovingkindness for those who love Him and keep His commandments,"[27]

Take the time to make sure your project has a **Vision** that is linked to a higher purpose. The higher purpose for Nehemiah was alignment with the will of God. You can see this in a number of places in the Scrolls which Nehemiah was familiar with why he was so committed and passionate about this higher purpose. For example:

> "Many plans are in a man's heart, But the counsel of the LORD will stand."[28]

> "The plans of the heart belong to man, But the answer of the tongue is from the LORD."[29]

> "The mind of man plans his way, But the LORD directs his steps."[30]

For Nehemiah, he did not consider himself to be in "control." He was obeying a higher calling. That higher calling is depicted in Psalm 127:

> "Unless the LORD builds the house, They labor in vain who build it; Unless the LORD guards the city, The watchman keeps awake in vain."[31]

It really comes down to the fact that Nehemiah understood all of these foundational principles discussed so far and in verses 4 – 10 he confesses the sin of the nation of Israel. He prayed. He fasted. He wept. He was 'all in'.

In verse 5 he sought God's heart in the matter and prayer and repentance was the foundation prior to any action by him. As we will see in Nehemiah chapter 2 verse 12 that he was listening to God, as well. Verse 8 back in chapter 1 tells us that Nehemiah knew the Word and the history of God's promises and, in agreement with those promises, prayed it back to God.

Verse 9 above reveals that Nehemiah had a plan in mind, but he knew the risk involved, so he asked God for favor with the earthly "champion" (or sponsor) – the king of Babylon–prior to the first project meeting. What a way to start a project! Most people would be running for the hills at this stage of the game (feet don't fail me now...). Instead, Nehemiah knew he could ask God for success and did so in verse 11:

> *11 O Lord, I beseech You, may Your ear be attentive to the prayer of Your servant and the prayer of Your servants who delight to revere Your name, and make Your servant successful today and grant him compassion before this man." Now I was the cupbearer to the king.*

We do not have a lot of historical data to give us an in depth understanding of the full role and responsibility of "the cupbearer" but there are only a few ever mentioned in any civilization. It is always a position of authority in close proximity to the ruler and likely involved staff as well as influence. Given what the king granted Nehemiah he was a key leader in the court of the king.

Nehemiah had a **Vision** that elevated him above his circumstances and that was aligned to a higher purpose, even though in order to accomplish that purpose, his life was literally on the line. It is always worth the effort to take the time to make sure your project has a **Vision** that is linked to a higher purpose. The higher purpose for Nehemiah was alignment with the will of God.

You can see this in a number of places in the Scrolls, or The Torah, which Nehemiah was familiar with and why he was so committed and passionate about this higher purpose.

Nehemiah Chapter 1 Action Steps

1. What needs to be clearly **Defined** in your project?
   a. Write those down and capture them as part of your project charter.
2. With whom do you need to **Distill** agreement.
   a. Document all agreements with your key stakeholders in meeting notes, etc.
3. Are there any impediments or obstacles to gaining agreement from internal or external stakeholders for your project.
   a. Create a Stakeholder Influence Map to assist you in communications and risk management.

NEHEMIAH 2

THE CHARTER

---

1 And it came about in the month Nisan, in the twentieth year of king Artaxerxes,

We are jumping into the middle of a verse here in order for you to see the time frame. Depending on when in the month of Chislev the news arrived and when in the month of Nisan Nehemiah went before the king it was between 3 and 4 months. Given the response Nehemiah gave king Artaxerxes he had already planned out what would be needed for a successful completion of Phase Two of the project to rebuild Jerusalem.

Planning had occurred so his answer was not off the cuff but well thought out and possibly even researched prior to this event. If you are going before an Executive you need to have a well thought out plan of action that the Executive can assess and decide on.

that wine was before him, and I took up the wine and gave it to the king. Now I had not been sad in his presence. 2 So the king said to me, "Why is your face sad though you are not sick? This is nothing but sadness of heart." Then I was very much afraid.

Nehemiah was justifiably afraid. If anyone approached the king with a sad face it was grounds for immediate death. This was not a small decision on the part of Nehemiah and he did not enter the king's presence with a sad face without knowing the potential consequence. Nehemiah was committed to this project even if it meant his own death. The possibility of death always brings clarity to project prioritization.

However, he knew that he was a favored person in the king's service and that his request was important to the queen, Esther, who was a Jew and who no doubt had influenced the king's earlier investment of over $3,000,000 in the refurbishing of the temple 13 years earlier.

He was asking to restart a failed part of the phase one of the project that had been stopped by order of a previous king. Ezra had gone back to complete the rebuilding of the Temple and had taken 13 years to complete the Temple. But, Ezra had not completed the walls and so the rebuilding of the walls portion of the project had not been done. We need to give Ezra some slack, though, since he was a Teacher of the Law, not an Executive, administrator or a project manager. We're fairly certain he was not a Certified PMP or ScrumMaster.

Every chapter gives us a new wow! We find in this verse that he was willing to die for the plan. Now that's commitment! How many project managers do you know that would be willing to die for their project? Talk about having some skin in the game. Nehemiah himself was in total agreement with the **Vision** of the project – to the point of being willing to die for it!

3 I said to the king, "Let the king live forever. Why should my face not be sad when the city, the place of my fathers' tombs, lies desolate and its gates have been consumed by fire?"

Define (D1) the problem.

4 Then the king said to me, "What would you request?" So I prayed to the God of heaven. 5 I said to the king, "If it please the king, and if your servant has found favor before you, send me to Judah, to the city of my fathers' tombs, that I may rebuild it."

Define (D1) the solution.

As we said before, it wasn't clear in Nehemiah's mind if he would survive the initial project request. In verse 3 he gives the problem statement and in verses 4 and 5 he gives the solution and indirectly mentions his past favor with the king and asks for a decree (Project Charter) to be issued to rebuild the walls of Jerusalem. This decree was issued March, 14 in the year 445 BCE according to historic documents, over 2,455 years ago.

Since **Definitions** should **Drive** everything that we do as project managers, then it is appropriate to have a **Definition** for the word "**Define:**"

"1 a: to determine or identify the essential qualities or meaning of <whatever defines

us as human> 1 b: to discover and set forth the meaning of (as a word) c: to create on a computer <define a window> <define a procedure>

2 a: to fix or mark the limits of : demarcate <rigidly defined property lines> 2 b: to make distinct, clear, or detailed especially in outline <the issues aren't too well defined>

3: characterize, distinguish <you define yourself by the choices you make — Denison University Bulletin> intransitive verb: to make a definition

— de·fine·ment \-⬚fin-m⬚nt\ noun
— de·fin·er \-⬚fi-n⬚r\ noun"[32 and 33]

Without clear and concise **Definitions** that are agreed to by all stakeholders, your project, program and/or portfolio will be exposed to unnecessary grief, issues, problems, risks, and corrective actions. Everyone on the team needs to quickly develop a common vocabulary and be singing from the same page of music. This is crucial when looking at the demand management processes that include requirements, specifications, etc.

Any time a **Definition** changes in your project, then you automatically have a change to your project scope. If you are experiencing run away projects, budget over-runs, schedule delays or scope creep, then it's clear that your **Definitions** have changed. This is the classic, "oh by the way" or "small change" that your end-user or client would like to make.

The second part of the **4D Model** is **Distill**. This is exactly as it sounds. The idea is to "cook" the **Definitions**, under pressure (allowing disagreement among the team members ... the only bad idea is the one not mentioned, etc.) so that you can get buy-in and agreement from ALL of the team members and/or Stakeholders.

With a clearly stated solution, you can **Distill** (**D2**) Agreement between the key stakeholders starting with Executive buy-in. The brevity of the request that follows is similar to what we might call a Project Charter with time frames and budgets and resources in today's world. Just enough to lay out the end result and the high level needs and budget.

Distillation is one key area in which many projects fail miserably. Instead of using disagreement, conflict and confrontation to improve the team as demonstrated in the "Tuckman" model (i.e. Forming → Storming → Norming → Performing → Adjourning),[34] many teams, both Agile and traditional, deal with uncomfortable, "storming" situations by throwing dissenting team members over the side of the boat.

Further, the **Distillation** process in the **UVF** is what prevents groupthink and is crucial for gaining agreement from your team.

Most project management methodologies have absolutely no check or balance in their methodologies to prevent groupthink (and then all of the negative consequences of having groupthink take over the team and the project). When projects fail, this is usually one of the areas that cause them to crash and burn. The **4D Model**, on the other hand, actually plugs this massive gap in all of the project management methodologies on the market today. That alone is worth its weight in gold. Just being "Agile" does not prevent groupthink.

Once you've **Defined** and **Distilled** your project, then **Delivering** (**D3**) becomes much, much easier than if you hadn't done the previous steps. Each and every organization has its various methods regarding creating and deploying projects, programs and port-folios, but most organizations do not manage the **Definition** and **Distillation** processes well enough to be able to **Deliver** the projects, on-time, on-budget, in-scope and within the quality and ROI (return on investment) expected.

We believe that this is why there's been such a dismal failure rate for so many projects for such a long time.

Driving (**D4**) the program, project, etc. includes all of the change management (people change man-agement is included here) and communication nec-essary to **Drive** the project home. Project Managers routinely underestimate the need for people change management and most are woefully prepared to do what's needed to implement the changes the project will create.

In the PMBOK Guide, version 5, (the Project Management Body of Knowledge published by PMI, the Project Management Institute) they have the 5 process areas (Initiate, Plan, Execute, Monitor & Control and Close). This almost mirrors our **4D Model**:

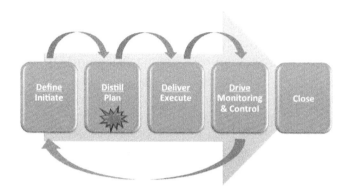

The PMBOK process areas can be put into an iterative format and can be viewed like we have in the following illustration:

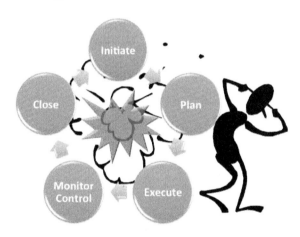

In fact, we recently encountered a company that actually had taken the PMBOK and put it in exactly the same iterative figure as above and called it Agile. Making it iterative and doing all of these at once, for them, is being Agile. In the PMBOK outline, we have moved the explosion (roughly equivalent to "**Distill**" in the **4D Model**) into the middle to show that it's really doing all 5 at once … it's like an explosion in the middle. Truly, your skill as a project manager/ScrumMaster is your ability to manage the explosion properly (the chaos in the middle) for the successful completion of your project.

> *6 Then the king said to me, the queen sitting beside him, "How long will your journey be, and when will you return?" So it pleased the king to send me, and I gave him a definite time.*

In verse 6 we see the executive sponsor requesting clarification and a **Definition** (**D1**). The **Sponsor** asked for a high-level project plan with time frames and budgets and resources. "I gave him a time" meant that Nehemiah actually had the high-level plan done in his head, at minimum, prior to bringing it to the executive level. Even though the rebuilding of the walls only took 52 days to complete, the actual time he was away from his role as the cupbearer for the king was 12 years (he moved from project leadership to governance). Nehemiah understood that he needed a project charter in order to deal with local stakeholders that had previously derailed the earlier project:

> *7 And I said to the king, "If it please the king, let letters be given me for the governors of the provinces beyond the River, that they may allow me to pass through until I come to Judah,*

The local rulers who had killed off this project before would need to have a letter from the king if Nehemiah was going to succeed. Risk planning and mitigation were practiced.

8 and a letter to Asaph the keeper of the king's forest, that he may give me timber to make beams for the gates of the fortress which is by the temple, for the wall of the city and for the house to which I will go." And the king granted them to me because the good hand of my God was on me.

Verse 8 in chapter 2 is an example of Nehemiah using **Distill** (**D2**) from the **4D Model** and includes **Agreement** and buy-in: the King agreed to Nehemiah's plan.

The first part of a plan that would be **Delivered** (**D3**) was planned prior to approaching the Executive for buy-in, or issuance of the Charter. With the letter from the king the balance of the planning and travel to the site (which would take a full year to complete) could then be started.

The decree was issued on March, 14 in the year 445 BCE according to historic documents, over 2,455 years ago. Verse 8 is an example of Nehemiah using the **Distill** (**D2**) from the **4D Model,** which includes **Agreement** with the **Definitions** (**D1**) and buy-in; the king agreed to Nehemiah's plan.

9 Then I came to the governors of the provinces beyond the River and gave them the king's letters. Now the king had sent with me officers of the army and horsemen.

The king was serious enough about the success of this project that he sent muscle and supporting documents (the letters to the Governors of the Trans-Euphrates) along with the administrator. We do not know how many Military personnel were with Nehemiah but we do know later in the book that there were 150 people who were being fed in his household. This was more than a token number of people and they were likely seasoned military leaders whom the king trusted. Our lesson for today is that even after a Charter is issued we need the Executive Sponsor for a project to send enough corporate muscle to **Drive** (**D4**) the project to a successful conclusion.

And in verse 9, **Deliver** (**D3**) commences imme-diately. The execution begins with clear Executive visibility (with the armed forces that accompanied Nehemiah) and support (the letters to the Governors of the Trans-Euphrates).

Nehemiah, either intuitively or intentionally, went through the **4D Model**. Nehemiah was not alone in rebuilding the walls of Jerusalem. He had a politically powerful project sponsor (i.e. the king of Babylon) along with the real project sponsor: *the* King (God).

As we looked at trying to do the organizational chart for this project, from the text it became clear quite quickly that this was no ordinary organiza-tional chart.

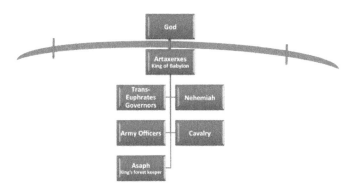

An amazing leaderhsip team was supporting Nehemiah! In verse 7 we have a Communication plan for the vendors as well as the direct and indirect stakeholders. It was part of the initial plan Nehemiah had ready. With that kind of backing and support, this project should have been a piece of cake, right? Not so fast.

10 When Sanballat the Horonite and Tobiah the Ammonite official heard about it, it was very displeasing to them that someone had come to seek the welfare of the sons of Israel.

Already in verse 10 we see the organizational (or cultural) immune system's "antibodies" rising up to oppose the plan. Any large initiative will have people or teams that oppose it. Here we see the same local cultural "antibodies" that succeeded in killing off the project a few years earlier rising up to oppose it again. Every organization has them, even yours. You may not even know who they are, but they are there.

Cultural "antibodies" are always a factor. For example, in Swedish we have the concept of "Jantelagen," that is, any stick that rises up out of a bundle will be hammered back into the stack by everyone else. We'll come back to how to deal with both of these types of "antibodies" (which can arise between **Deliver** and **Drive**, or even sooner) a little bit later in this book.

Verse 11 – 15 take us into the "Execution" of the plan at the project site. Nehemiah was following the iterative **4D Model** and we find the initial assessment **Definition (D1)** by Nehemiah with the starting status and condition prior to the first team meeting. The first meeting had a minimum of 42 representatives present. This would have required some amazing facilitation skills on Nehemiah's part.

11 So I came to Jerusalem and was there three days. 12 And I arose in the night, I and a few men with me. I did not tell anyone what my God was putting into my mind to do for Jerusalem and there was no animal with me except the animal on which I was riding.

In verse 12 it's clear that Nehemiah was listening to the voice of God the Father as well ("God put it into his heart..."). So the plan was "inspired," literally God-breathed.[35]

13 So I went out at night by the Valley Gate in the direction of the Dragon's Well and on to the Refuse Gate, inspecting the walls of

Jerusalem which were broken down and its gates which were consumed by fire. 14 Then I passed on to the Fountain Gate and the King's Pool, but there was no place for my mount to pass. 15 So I went up at night by the ravine and inspected the wall. Then I entered the Valley Gate again and returned.

In verses 16 -17 we have **Distill** (**D2**) underway with Nehemiah obtaining team buy-in, i.e. "let us." Team buy-in is crucial to the success of any project.

The level to which the organization allows the teams to self organize is dependent upon the leader's skill and comfort level in delegating power to the teams. It's interesting that even in a hierarchical monarchy where chain of command would have been enforced quite severely, that we find such a breath of fresh "Agile" air in Nehemiah's approach. The good news here is that if you are constrained by a top-down, functional organization you can still use and implement a very Agile approach and achieve remarkable results.

16 The officials did not know where I had gone or what I had done; nor had I as yet told the Jews, the priests, the nobles, the officials or the rest who did the work.

D1 – Iteration inspection and validation. Nehemiah had planned the Charter, obtained Executive buy-in and worked on the plan and the materials preparation needed to do the project work based on hear-say evidence and narrative stories. Now that he was at the site he did an on the ground assessment to line up the actual facts with what he had been told (and believed to be true … "Inspection" is one of the three pillars of Scrum. The other two being transparency and adaptation.).

Nehemiah now establishes the **project Vision** (rebuilding the walls) in verse 17 and brings the **Vision** to a **personal level** (so that they might no longer live in disgrace):

17 Then I said to them, "You see the bad situation we are in, that Jerusalem is desolate and its gates burned by fire. Come, let us rebuild the wall of Jerusalem so that we will no longer be a reproach."

Nehemiah establishes an "Us" attitude. He did not dictate, "here is the plan now you guys do it." This is Good to Great "Level 5" servant leadership in action.[36] He had an "I am here to help" and a "we, together that will do this work" approach. A great example of pulling a team via leadership verses pushing a team via demands as pictured in the graphic below:

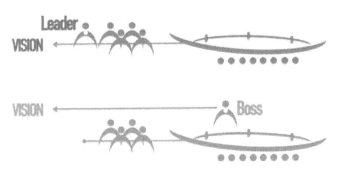

In verse 18 we see him employing the use of a "tribal story" in order to encourage, build confidence and the expectation of success (i.e. a personal testimony of "...can you believe what God did for us?!!! I thought I was going to get into huge trouble with the king, even to the point of losing my life; but, instead the king has sponsored this project!!!"). What's your project's "tribal story?" Does it have one? Does it need one?

> *18 I told them how the hand of my God had been favorable to me and also about the king's words which he had spoken to me.*

Nehemiah had stated the problem and now explains his Charter and the level of Executive buy-in. He uses a tribal story about the favor of the king to paint the **Vision** and alignment with that **Vision** for what needs to be done. Stories can be effectively used to build culture and team buy-in.

> *Then they said, "Let us arise and build." So they put their hands to the good work.*

In the second half of verse 18 we come to **Deliver** (**D3**); "So they began this good work." He now has team buy-in and they start the execution phase or enter into **Delivering** the product as **Defined** in the Charter.

We see that, as soon as they start, the same corporate "antibodies" that reared their ugly heads in verse 10 pop up again. Sanballat and the rest were attempting in verse 19 to suggest that Nehemiah didn't have a valid project charter:

19 But when Sanballat the Horonite and Tobiah the Ammonite official, and Geshem the Arab heard it, they mocked us and despised us and said, "What is this thing you are doing? Are you rebelling against the king?"

This is the same argument they had used to stall the project many years prior. However, this time, one of the king's trusted leaders was heading up the project so Nehemiah could confidently respond to the "antibodies." He had already asked for (and received) letters of approval to all of the Governors of the Trans-Euphrates. His Charter gave him the full authority of the Executive office. Sanballat and his friends were stopped short in their new efforts to derail the project. The lessons learned or retrospective from the previous project failure allowed Nehemiah to plan for these risks and to mitigate them in advance.

20 So I answered them and said to them, "The God of heaven will give us success; therefore we His servants will arise and build, but you have no portion, right or memorial in Jerusalem."

How many times have you experienced that once you get your project going and are **Delivering** the product, service or result that suddenly another "stakeholder," that had been asleep at the switch, suddenly comes to life and interferes?

Understanding how to manage Political realities, while creating team unity and building critical mass, will often determine the success or failure of your project.

Actually, it's interesting to note that Nehemiah declared Sanballat a non-stakeholder for the project in verse 20: "but as for you, you have no share in Jerusalem or any claim or historic right to it."

Nehemiah declared Sanballat's attempt to participate and/or influence the teams as "out-of-scope" to the project; and, at the same time he **planned for the risks** posed by this external interference from Sanballat and set up contingency plans to mitigate those risks.

Nehemiah Chapter 2 Action Steps

1. Take a minute to reflect on the **4D Model** and how it might be applied in your organization.
2. As a leader, do you push or do you pull?
3. What can you do right now to establish a lead-by-example (i.e. pull) dynamic within your team structure?

DISTILLED AGREEMENTS & COMMUNICATION

———

T his chapter is a total game-changer! Chapter 3 is a list of all of the teams, team leaders, groups and stakeholders involved in the implementation of one of the largest scaled Agile projects ever attempted. If you want to **scale Agile to 50,000 team members, or beyond,** then you will definitely have to think outside of the box like Nehemiah did.

> *1 Then Eliashib the high priest arose with his brothers the priests and built the Sheep Gate; they consecrated it and hung its doors. They consecrated the wall to the Tower of the Hundred and the Tower of Hananel. 2 Next to him the men of Jericho built, and next to them Zaccur the son of Imri built.*

> *3 Now the sons of Hassenaah built the Fish Gate; they laid its beams and hung its doors*

with its bolts and bars. 4 Next to them Meremoth the son of Uriah the son of Hakkoz made repairs. And next to him Meshullam the son of Berechiah the son of Meshezabel made repairs. And next to him Zadok the son of Baana also made repairs. 5 Moreover, next to him the Tekoites made repairs, but their nobles did not support the work of their masters.

6 Joiada the son of Paseah and Meshullam the son of Besodeiah repaired the Old Gate; they laid its beams and hung its doors with its bolts and its bars. 7 Next to them Melatiah the Gibeonite and Jadon the Meronothite, the men of Gibeon and of Mizpah, also made repairs for the official seat of the governor of the province beyond the River. 8 Next to him Uzziel the son of Harhaiah of the goldsmiths made repairs. And next to him Hananiah, one of the perfumers, made repairs, and they restored Jerusalem as far as the Broad Wall.

Nehemiah demonstrated servant leadership and led by example. Many of the other leaders did the same. Actually in this chapter we find a number of rulers, or ruler's sons directly involved in the rebuilding efforts:

9 Next to them Rephaiah the son of Hur, the official of half the district of Jerusalem, made repairs. 10 Next to them Jedaiah the son of Harumaph made repairs opposite his house. And next to him Hattush the son of Hashabneiah made repairs. 11 Malchijah the son of Harim and Hasshub the son of Pahath-moab repaired another section and the Tower of Furnaces. 12 Next to him Shallum the son of Hallohesh, the official of half the district of Jerusalem, made repairs, he and his daughters.

13 Hanun and the inhabitants of Zanoah repaired the Valley Gate. They built it and hung its doors with its bolts and its bars, and a thousand cubits of the wall to the Refuse Gate.

14 Malchijah the son of Rechab, the official of the district of Beth-haccherem repaired the Refuse Gate. He built it and hung its doors with its bolts and its bars.

15 Shallum the son of Col-hozeh, the official of the district of Mizpah, repaired the Fountain Gate. He built it, covered it and hung its doors with its bolts and its bars, and the wall of the Pool of Shelah at the king's garden as far as the steps that descend from the city of David.

Verses 1 through 15 demonstrate one of the first times in history that the idea of **self-organizing teams** appears. Not only that, but in verse 16 we find an Executive working right alongside the team:

16 After him Nehemiah the son of Azbuk, official of half the district of Beth-zur, made repairs as far as a point opposite the tombs of David, and as far as the artificial pool and the house of the mighty men.

17 After him the Levites carried out repairs under Rehum the son of Bani. Next to him Hashabiah, the official of half the district of Keilah, carried out repairs for his district. 18 After him their brothers carried out repairs under Bavvai the son of Henadad, official of the other half of the district of Keilah. 19 Next to him Ezer the son of Jeshua, the official of Mizpah, repaired another section in front of the ascent of the armory at the Angle. 20 After him Baruch the son of Zabbai zealously repaired another section, from the Angle to the doorway of the house of Eliashib the high priest. 21 After him Meremoth the son of Uriah the son of Hakkoz repaired another section, from the doorway of Eliashib's house even as far as the end of his house. 22 After him the priests, the men of the valley, carried out repairs. 23 After them Benjamin and Hasshub carried out repairs in front of their house. After them Azariah the son of Maaseiah, son of Ananiah, carried out repairs beside his house. 24 After him Binnui the son of Henadad repaired another section, from the house of Azariah as far as the Angle and as far as the corner. 25 Palal the son of Uzai made repairs in front of the Angle and the tower projecting from the upper house of the king, which is by the court of the guard. After him Pedaiah the son of Parosh made repairs. 26 The temple servants living in Ophel made repairs as far as the front of the Water Gate toward the east and the projecting tower. 27 After them the Tekoites repaired another section in front of the great projecting tower and as far as the wall of Ophel.

28 Above the Horse Gate the priests carried out repairs, each in front of his house. 29 After them Zadok the son of Immer carried out repairs in front of his house. And after him Shemaiah the son of Shecaniah, the keeper of the East Gate, carried out repairs. 30 After him Hananiah the son of Shelemiah, and Hanun the sixth son of Zalaph, repaired another section. After him Meshullam the son of Berechiah carried out repairs in front of his own quarters. 31 After him Malchijah, one of the goldsmiths, carried out repairs as far as the house of the temple servants and of the merchants, in front of the Inspection Gate and as far as the upper room of the corner. 32 Between the upper room of the corner and the Sheep Gate the goldsmiths and the merchants carried out repairs.

What a beautiful picture of "Level 5" servant leadership. For these leaders it was more than just talking the talk. It was walking the talk.

We once worked on a project at a large Fortune 500 organization in the US and we noticed that a team member had been placing a check mark next to each of the organization's core values on the poster in his cubicle. Finally, Ted asked him one day, "what are all of the check marks for?" The team member chuckled and responded, "oh, the check marks are for each time one of the executives violates one of the core values."

The poster, sadly, was full of multiple check marks next to each "core value" by which the organization claimed it lived. There wasn't a single core value that hadn't been violated, multiple times. A person is only as good as their word and if as a leader they violate core principles people take notice. It creates organization dissonance and mistrust.

As a Product Owner, ScrumMaster or project manager, never, ever make a promise that you either can't or don't intend on keeping. Say anything, but don't make promises that you can't fulfill (for whatever reason). If for any reason you cannot keep a promise be transparent and go immediately to the affected Stakeholders to explain why this promise can no longer be kept. Then lay out what steps are being taken to mitigate the impacts.

In this chapter we are given the high-level WBS (work breakdown structure), also known as a Product Backlog in Agile:

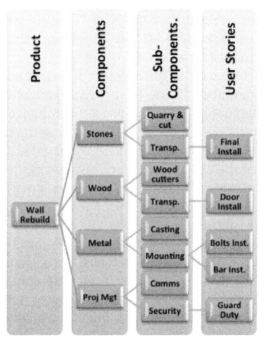

Each of the teams, for their section of the wall, would have to have self-organized into some kind of WBS (Work Breakdown Structure) or a PBL (Prioritized Product Backlog), like the one above. Of course, the above WBS/PBL is simplified and assumes that their logistics enabled the right materials would be at the right locations as needed. For example; that there was mortar available for the installation of the stones; that the hardware (metal parts) could be cast on-site; and that there were wagons and animals enough to pull those wagons for resource transportation purposes; that there were enough tools and weapons on hand.

Was there was enough food and provisions to feed the hungry (and eventually very tired) army that was building (and defending the building) of the wall? Ever tried to feed 10 people at a dinner? 100? 500? Try visualizing the 7.5 weeks of rations that would have been necessary to feed almost 50,000 people and over 8,000 animals. That is truly mind-boggling!

Now, before all of my Agile friends get upset with the Figure above; simply substitute "Epic" for the "Components" level. Substitute "Product Backlog Items" (i.e. User Stories) for the Sub-component level (the "User Story" level corresponds, roughly, to the "Work Package" level in Traditional methodologies. Viola! You now have an Agile/Scrum structure.

For those of you making the transition from Waterfall to Scrum, this is an easy way to correlate what you used to do with the new way of thinking (which, as demonstrated by Nehemiah, isn't so new after all).

It has quickly become clear in many of the agile project management communities of practice that traditional project hierarchies really don't work (however, people still try). It didn't work for Nehemiah, either. After trying to put together (or trying to use) a standard organizational chart to help visualize the teams that rebuilt the walls we were presented with some real "opportunities" (like our brother Dan, except for Tsunamis, we do not recognize the existence of "problems," only "opportunities"), until we found another way to represent the chart.

What worked, in the end, was a "long chain" that had been linked to a common **Vision** and that had the buy-in and agreement of the teams **Delivering** the final product, service or result (in this case, the new walls and gates for Jerusalem). Each team was responsible for a small increment of the end result. It worked out to roughly 565 feet per team. The total length of the wall was 4.5 miles. This works out to just over one-tenth of a mile per team / team leader (about 0.107 mile per team).

Here's what the "chain" for the Builders of the Wall from Nehemiah chapter 3 (each box represents a team of builders and all of the teams together were "**Nehemiah Agile**") looked like:

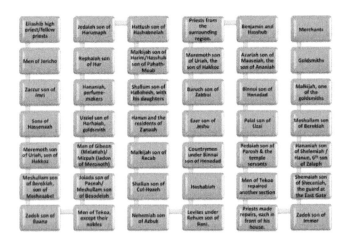

It's interesting that some of the teams had "named" team leaders and other teams didn't. Some of the teams did multiple sections of the work. Nehemiah began with the priests (the spiritual foundation) and ended with the goldsmiths and merchants (the business process guys).

One of the teams still got the job done, even though their leadership (the "nobles") refused to put their shoulders to the work. Did the teams accomplish this by overthrowing the leaders that refused to get involved? No, but they finished the work despite the complete lack of support from their leadership. Bad leadership is never an excuse for not getting the job done. **Define** the blockers, adapt, adjust and move on to completing the project **Vision**.

Years ago, we worked on a project for a very large Fortune 500 organization where we coined the phrase, "when cross-functional expectations were not realized, we took the following steps to accomplish our goals." Sometimes you just have to find a way to get it done, regardless of the amount of help that you do, or do not, receive from other groups or even your own leaders.

It is clear that these teams working on the wall were the epitome of self-organizing ... especially the ones that had no team leaders or executive support! They were Agile in the deepest sense of the word.

The work was completed in September, so they worked long, hard days in the middle of the summer with a load of bricks in one hand and their sword or spear in the other to fend off the political "anti-bodies" (sounds like many of the projects on which we've worked). The temperatures at that time of the year in Israel run between 85 to 100 degrees Fahrenheit with fairly high humidity. There were 49,942 people working on the project. That works out to 1,189 per team on the average for the 42 teams involved. Even with today's technology, this would be a stunning achievement, let alone doing it manually under harsh conditions 2,500 years ago!

How do you motivate and manage that many people (who were volunteers) in that type of environment? It was the **Vision** that drew the whole project together. Nehemiah's organizational structure for the project was pure genius, but without the compelling **Vision**, he would not have accomplished this amazing result.

If we stretched this line of teams out and follow the original walls, you would have a map of the walls of Jerusalem as reconstructed by Nehemiah and the teams.

Doesn't sound so complicated, does it? But, from a communications standpoint, this was a very challenging situation for Nehemiah. Using the communications channel formula (found in the PMBOK):

(n*(n-1))/2

This worked out to a potential 903 channels for each of the 42 team leaders plus Nehemiah (43*(43-1)/2. But, because of the simple communication structure that Nehemiah used, it really worked out to only 2 external channels per team. There were roughly 42 teams, so there were around 84 channels per team leader, a reduction of over 90% in the communication channels needed to get the job done!

Now, combine that with the concept that 80 – 90% of ALL project management involves communications, and you'll start to understand the genius of what Nehemiah had done.

This picture shows how Nehemiah achieved a major breakthrough in communications of truly amazing proportions:

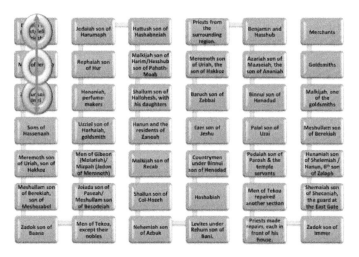

As shown in figure above, since each group was working on a single section of the wall, for proper integration to take place each team only needed to communicate with the team on either side of their immediate group, thus reducing the communication channels significantly.

This, in a nutshell, is how you scale an agile project. The organizational communications format that Nehemiah created was simple and elegant. It was amazingly effective.

Simple communication channels free the organization from the complexities that weigh it down and that can cause unweildy complexity that makes communication almost impossible.

Nehemiah Chapter 3 Action Steps

1. Do you need to reduce the number of touch points in order to increase the effetiveness of your communications?
2. Identify all potential communication bottlenecks for your project.
   a. Which of those bottlenecks can be eliminated or mitigated?
3. What is the "trumpet" that will simplify your communication channels?

DELIVER THE ITERATIVE PLAN BY RESPONDING TO CHANGE

I t didn't take very long into the project before Nehemiah encountered some fierce opposition. The project's enemies rose up from outside of the project, again, and this time Nehemiah chooses the path of ignoring his detractors and instead he focuses on **Delivery (D4)**. Daniel Burrus would call this "Skipping your biggest problem."[37]

Chapter 4 in Nehemiah records for us the reaction of Sanballat and the enemies of God:

1 Now it came about that when Sanballat heard that we were rebuilding the wall, he became furious and very angry and mocked the Jews. 2 He spoke in the presence of his brothers and the wealthy men of Samaria and said, "What are these feeble Jews doing? Are they going to restore it for themselves? Can they offer sacrifices? Can they finish in a day? Can they revive the stones from the dusty rubble even the burned ones?" 3 Now Tobiah the Ammonite was near him and he said, "Even what they are building—if a fox should jump on it, he would break their stone wall down!"

Don't know about you, but we haven't had a project yet where (usually somewhere halfway through the project) a "Sanballat" hasn't jumped out of the woodwork to oppose the project and the product, service or result that we were trying to produce. We already saw in a previous chapter that Sanballat tried to use fear and intimidation to prevent Nehemiah's teams from even starting the project by injecting "politics" by suggesting that Nehemiah and the leadership were somehow rebelling against the king of Babylon (i.e. that they didn't have a proper Project Charter). Instead, Nehemiah rebuked Sanballat and his enemies and moved forward with the project.

If you ever want to stop a project in its tracks, the best thing that you can do is to sow confusion among the project team. A babel approach. It is a tactic that is simple, yet rather effective.

Sanballat seemed to understand this because he attacked the project's idea and **Vision**, once again, basically declaring it a "mission impossible" and Tobiah attacked the quality of the construction (the final product). This time Nehemiah only prayed and returned Sanballat and Tobiah's curses back on their own heads. This was exhibiting extremely wise leadership on Nehemiah's part. It is not necessary to respond to every objection that is raised against your project. Let the final product speak for itself.

Drive Success via Inspection and Adaptation

Sometimes there is an "explosion" that happens between **Deliver** (**D3**) and **Drive** (**D4**) and you will need to use the **4D Model** to mitigate this as illustrated in the following figures. The explosion is usually triggered by an "oh by the way."

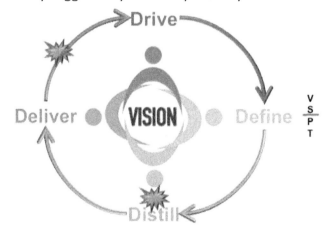

If we were to follow PMBOK's traditional change control methodology, it would have us do the change control inside the project as shown in the following picture:

TRADITIONAL CHANGE CONTROL

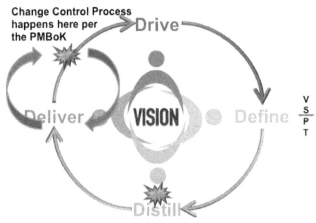

But, that is only part of the story, since strictly following the PMBOK could risk losing Stakeholder buy-in and unity due to the change. Making any iterative changes to the original project plan and/ or Charter without taking that change back through the filter of the project **Vision** risks a loss of unity that can easily be avoided. This prevents you from getting mired down or distracted by 'non-**Vision**' focused changes in the project **Delivery** and thus potentially sacrificing the team's velocity or success.

ONLY PART OF THE STORY

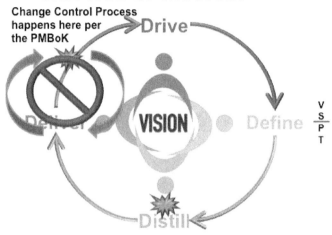

Change Control Process happens here per the PMBoK

Drive

VISION

Define

Deliver

Distill

V
S
P
T

We have found that if you really want to make the iterative **4D Model** work, you have to take any proposed change back to the start. Go to the beginning and filter the change against the original **Vision** and business purpose. That can be done in as little as a 15 minute stand-up meeting and that's the rest of the story:

THE REST OF THE STORY

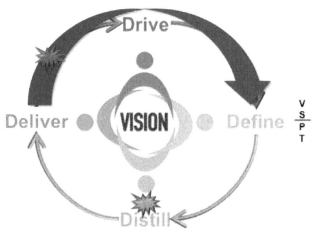

The **4D Model** is iterative and can be used with any project management methodology to mitigate scope creep or uncontrolled Product Backlog growth. It is an effective tool for continuous prioritization.

Nehemiah first dealt with the non-stakeholder (Sanballat) challenges via **communication**; and, as well find later on in Nehemiah chapter 4 verses 1-6, he eventually simply prayed and did not communicate with the non-stakeholder. And that brings us to the next section on the Effect of Proper Communications.

4 Hear, O our God, how we are despised! Return their reproach on their own heads and give them up for plunder in a land of captivity. 5 Do not forgive their iniquity and

let not their sin be blotted out before You, for
they have demoralized the builders.

Sometimes to you have to break out the big artillery in order to win the war. In fact, Nehemiah used the external attack against the teams building the wall into a motivator for the teams:

6 So we built the wall and the whole wall
was joined together to half its height, for the
people had a mind to work.

This was a **Project Milestone:** "half its height." In some translations, "the people had a mind to work" can be interpreted "had a whole heart to work." The teams were motivated to the point of exhaustion, with nothing held back to accomplish the task of rebuilding the walls.

One of the key meetings in Scrum is the **Sprint Review / Product Demonstartion** at the end of a sprint. Here, in a construction project you have a demonstration at a milestone that could be used to encourage and motivate the team to completion.

Think about it. What would your project look like if the entire team "worked with all their heart?" The results would truly be remarkable. In other words they had taken personal ownership for the results and had rebuilt the walls to half its height. Already remarkable results had been achieved and they were not even done, yet. Talk about pouring salt in Sanballat's wounds! But, Sanballat wasn't about to sit still, either:

7 Now when Sanballat, Tobiah, the Arabs, the Ammonites and the Ashdodites heard that the repair of the walls of Jerusalem went on, and that the breaches began to be closed, they were very angry. 8 All of them conspired together to come and fight against Jerusalem and to cause a disturbance in it.

The opposition had intensified. Therefore, a stronger response and **Risk action plan** was put into motion (backed-up by prayer) plus a modification of the scope of the work effort to reflect the need for protection and project security. This is a change to the project scope in the middle of the sprint with the part of the resources being diverted to managing the politics of the situation.

Politics can make or break your project.

It is the responsibility of the project sponsor to provide the political cover to the teams (remember the letters Nehemiah had for the all of the Trans-Euphrates governors along with the troops to back him up?). Nehemiah new he had the full support of the Ultimate Stakeholder (God) as well as the organizational Champion (the king). Now that's some political cover!

9 But we prayed to our God, and because of them we set up a guard against them day and night.

What's amazing to us is that Sanballat just doesn't seem like the brightest candle on the cake, does he?

Didn't he understand that the king of Babylon had sponsored the project? Maybe he understood it at some level, but it seems clear that Sanballat had a personal agenda and so he used some psychological warfare on the teams when they were at the point of physical exhaustion:

> *10 Thus in Judah it was said,*
> *"The strength of the burden bearers is failing,*
> *Yet there is much rubbish;*
> *And we ourselves are unable*
> *To rebuild the wall."*

He used tactical mind games against the teams:

> *11 Our enemies said, "They will not know or see until we come among them, kill them and put a stop to the work."*

The teams were tired and the enemy was getting into their heads by continually bombarding them with new information:

> *12 When the Jews who lived near them came and told us ten times, "They will come up against us from every place where you may turn,"*

Now that's some major meddling from someone external to the project that had no legitimate claim, stake or say in the final product. Nehemiah responded to Sanballat's meddling by refocusing the teams on the **Vision** of the project:

13 then I stationed men in the lowest parts of the space behind the wall, the exposed places, and I stationed the people in families with their swords, spears and bows. 14 When I saw their fear, I rose and spoke to the nobles, the officials and the rest of the people: "Do not be afraid of them; remember the Lord who is great and awesome, and fight for your brothers, your sons, your daughters, your wives and your houses."

Verses 13 and 14 share the scope change (altering the scope of the project plan) by going back to **Define** (**D1**) and Nehemiah confronted the brutal facts (we're all going to die if we don't take a stand). Nehemiah immediately moved to **Distill** (**D2**) with the teams to gain a new agreement. Nehemiah knew that it was time for the gloves to come off and take the enemy out of the equation. Nehemiah reminded the teams who they had as their **ultimate Stakeholder** (God, great and awesome) and that they all had **skin in the game** (fight for your brothers, your sons and your daughters, your wives and your homes) and realigned the leaders and team members with the **Vision** and the prudence of the changes to the plan.

Nehemiah was basically answering the main question every team member had: "**hey dude, what's in it for me?**" He brought the teams back to personal buy-in and agreement. Survival is a powerful motivator and it wouldn't be too hard to gain agreement that survival is preferable to the alternative. If not for yourself, then at least for your families. Nehemiah understood this as a leader since he had risked death himself early on to initiate this project.

With **D1** and **D2** back on track, Nehemiah could get the teams focused back on **Delivery** (**D3**):

15 When our enemies heard that it was known to us, and that God had frustrated their plan, then all of us returned to the wall, each one to his work.

The **4D Model** is a powerful, iterative weapon to immediately deal with the changing landscape in your projects, agile or otherwise. Nehemiah did this intuitively. It brought the project back into alignment and allowed Nehemiah to get back to **Driving** (**D4**):

16 From that day on, half of my servants carried on the work while half of them held the spears, the shields, the bows and the breastplates; and the captains were behind the whole house of Judah. 17 Those who were rebuilding the wall and those who carried burdens took their load with one hand doing the work and the other holding a weapon. 18 As for the builders, each wore his sword girded at his side as he built, while the trumpeter stood near me.

Nehemiah had successfully adjusted the project, mid-stream, to mitigate the changes in the external environment and redeployed the resources accordingly. We need to teach our teams how to fight. We need to arm them, too. OK, maybe not with actual swords and spears, but at least the modern business equivalent. How often have you, as a project manager, been sent into a deep, dark cave and the only tool that management has given you to slay the monster is a flashlight? Did we mention the monster has sharp teeth, is angry and hungry?

The other thing Nehemiah did was to limit the communication to the other leaders. The secret here is to only give the other Steering Committee (or Group) members just the information that they need for that moment. In fact, he only used one tool: the trumpet.

19 I said to the nobles, the officials and the rest of the people, "The work is great and extensive, and we are separated on the wall far from one another. 20 At whatever place you hear the sound of the trumpet, rally to us there. Our God will fight for us."

Only raise the alarm for the risk(s) that actually materialize, martial the troops to focus on and defeat the problem at hand, and then return back to your daily project work. Plan for the risks and strategize how to respond appropriately but don't waste your time worrying about what might happen or materialize.

This is pure genius on Nehemiah's part to take the channels of communication down to one: the trumpet. This is the only way to be truly agile on a scaled project of this magnitude: identify your "trumpet," the simple communication signals that you will use and how to focus the teams only on the risks that can sink the project. Nothing else.

That is Agile risk management at its finest.

He returned to and reinforced this with the original **Vision**: "Our God will fight for us!" And Nehemiah knew that **Vision** alone isn't enough to keep the teams going, especially when they're already exhausted half-way through the project. In verse 21 it's clear that sometimes an extra effort (i.e. crashing) is needed to pull the project off, they worked early to late (overtime is always the preferred method of crashing as compared to adding additional resources to the project). Besides, Nehemiah already had a finite number of people on the teams and no additional resources were going to be available.

21 So we carried on the work with half of them holding spears from dawn until the stars appeared.

These guys were putting in 16-hour days on the walls both building and defending it, and it didn't end there:

22 At that time I also said to the people, "Let each man with his servant spend the night within Jerusalem so that they may be a guard for us by night and a laborer by day." 23 So neither I, my brothers, my servants, nor the men of the guard who followed me, none of us removed our clothes, each took his weapon even to the water.

Nehemiah led by example. Superb servant leadership was being demonstrated. His walk and his talk matched. If you want your teams to follow you to the death, then this is an amazing example of how to get over-the-cliff loyalty from your team members. Not only were they working on the walls by day, they were guarding the city by night and Nehemiah was leading in a real, tangible and visible way.

This project was so intense that they didn't even take the time to take their clothes off at night and they were armed and ready for action 24x7. For 52 days (almost 7.5 weeks) straight! Now that's intense. One **language**, one **mind**, one **plan** came together by means of a **Unified Vision**. Having a common, external enemy **unified** the teams.

That's powerful, powerful wisdom.

Nehemiah Chapter 4 Action Steps

1. Have you mapped the actual problem you project solves?
   a. What benefit will it **Deliver**
   b. How will you measure its success?
2. Is Executive buy-in strong or weak for your project?

    a. How will your planning or the execution of your plan change as a result of this knowledge?

3. Have you set aside time in your planning to identify potential enemies to the project?

    a. What strategies will you employ to deal with these threats?

4. Are you a Level 5 Servant Leader or are you more comfortable with a command and control structure trying to rule via demands?

    a. What steps can you take today to change this?

5. Do you take care to follow through on your promises? Are you known as a trustworthy person who does what they say they will do?

    a. If not what steps can you take today to become more trustworthy?

6. Are all the logistical needs of your team dealt with?

7. Do you have a visual representation of the project and the project team to assist in communication?

8. Do you currently work hard to establish and maintain focus on the project **Vision**?

    a. If not, why not?

    b. What steps could you take today to begin **Delivering** this focus?

    c. Do you have a simple tool that will help you with this task?

9. Have you clearly **Defined** the Product Backlog? Does every team member

understand their portion of the project "wall" that is their responsibility?

    a. If not, stop everything and gain that clarity before trying to complete your project. Trouble lies ahead if you do not.

10. What simple tool will you use to communicate real risks to your Stakeholders and key leaders?

    a. What templates should your project NOT use to get the project done?

    b. Is your PMO prepared to take templates away from the project teams that are actually obstacles to getting the projects done?

MANAGING THE TEAM

I f in the previous chapter we saw how an external enemy unified the team behind the **Vision**, in Chapter 5 of Nehemiah, we will look at the enemy that arises from within the project. After Chapter 4 of Nehemiah you would be tempted to assume that everything went according to plan. How many of you have ever had a project go exactly according to plan? General George Patton once said that no plan has survived the first five minutes of battle. It was no different for Nehemiah. The leadership that he displays in this chapter is second-to-none. It is amazing.

1 Now there was a great outcry of the people and of their wives against their Jewish brothers. 2 For there were those who said, "We, our sons and our daughters are many; therefore let us get grain that we may eat and live." 3 There were others who said, "We are mortgaging our fields, our vineyards and our houses that we might get grain because of the famine." 4 Also there were those who said, "We have borrowed money for the king's tax on our fields and our vineyards. 5 Now our flesh is like the flesh of our brothers, our children like their children. Yet behold, we are forcing our sons and our daughters to be slaves, and some of our daughters are forced into bondage already, and we are helpless because our fields and vineyards belong to others."

Not only were there external enemies that Nehemiah had to deal with, he had to deal with lousy weather (verse 3) and a famine as well. Without food, it's hard to keep the army fighting or a construction crew working. People had to pay a high premium just to get grain for their daily bread and were taking out loans on their land, crops and property in order to get by. Worse, it will later be revealed that it was their own leaders who were taking advantage of the situation and loaning the money in the tight times, and the were charging interest on the loans (which, under Mosaic law, was not allowed).

Because of the heavy taxes the king of Babylon was levying on the subjects, they had to sell their children into slavery in order to pay their taxes since they no longer owned their homes, land or crops. Rather dire circumstances for the team members and no light at the end of the tunnel.

Nehemiah's leadership response to this was correct and one more time, he had to use the **4D Model**, but this time inside the team:

6 Then I was very angry when I had heard their outcry and these words.

The **Definitions** had changed for the teams members due to the famine **Define** (**D1**). And Nehemiah understood that he needed to move to **Distill** (**D2**) in order to evoke a very needed change.

Sometimes the right response is anger. Especially when it comes to injustices committed against the teams. Before responding, Nehemiah thought about it (i.e. he consulted himself) and then nailed the offenders to the wall:

7 I consulted with myself and contended with the nobles and the rulers and said to them, "You are exacting usury, each from his brother!" Therefore, I held a great assembly against them. 8 I said to them, "We according to our ability have redeemed our Jewish brothers who were sold to the nations; now would you even sell your brothers that they may be sold to us?" Then they were silent and could not find a word to say.

The confrontation on these issues was in-person, with the nobles (the leaders). Nehemiah nailed the nobles with a commonly agreed to **Definition** (God's) regarding usury from one's countryman. He confronted them regarding their slave trade, which was against the commonly agreed to **Definition** from the Bible. What could the nobles say?

Nehemiah had them dead to rights. We were taught that silence is equal to **agreement**. Silence is the same as saying "yes." The local leaders knew that they had gotten caught with their hands in the cookie jar. Although the leaders were left speechless and in shame, Nehemiah wasn't done:

> *9 Again I said, "The thing which you are doing is not good; should you not walk in the fear of our God because of the reproach of the nations, our enemies? 10 And likewise I, my brothers and my servants are lending them money and grain. Please, let us leave off this usury. 11 Please, give back to them this very day their fields, their vineyards, their olive groves and their houses, also the hundredth part of the money and of the grain, the new wine and the oil that you are exacting from them."*

Nehemiah forced the officials to return the team member's land, crops and home and to stop charging them interest on the loans **Deliver (D3)**. And Nehemiah walked the talk, he didn't just talk the talk ... he and his brothers and men were making interest free loans (they put their money where their mouths were). The result of this leadership was the right response on the part of the nobles:

> *12 Then they said, "We will give it back and will require nothing from them; we will do exactly as you say." So I called the priests and*

took an oath from them that they would do according to this promise.

In the second half of verse 12 Nehemiah gained a new agreement (**D2**) from the officials (officials took an oath). In verses 12 – 13 above we see that Nehemiah achieved **Driving (D4)** to success because the people actually did as they had promised.

13 I also shook out the front of my garment and said, "Thus may God shake out every man from his house and from his possessions who does not fulfill this promise; even thus may he be shaken out and emptied." And all the assembly said, "Amen!" And they praised the Lord. Then the people did according to this promise.

14 Moreover, from the day that I was appointed to be their governor in the land of Judah, from the twentieth year to the thirty-second year of king Artaxerxes, for twelve years, neither I nor my kinsmen have eaten the governor's food allowance. 15 But the former governors who were before me laid burdens on the people and took from them bread and wine besides forty shekels of silver; even their servants domineered the people. But I did not do so because of the fear of God. 16 I also applied myself to the work on this wall; we did not buy any land, and all my servants were gathered there for the work.

Anyone that has done their PMP Certification will immediately recognize what Nehemiah did from a Code of Conduct perspective. The Project Management Institute Code of Ethics and Professional Conduct states in the following sections:

"2.2.1 We make decisions and take actions based on the best interests of society, public safety, and the environment.

3.3.2 We do not exercise the power of our expertise or position to influence the decisions or actions of others in order to benefit personally at their expense.

5.3.2 We do not engage in dishonest behavior with the intention of personal gain or at the expense of another."[38]

Nehemiah simply refused to benefit from the project at the expense of the other team members.

17 Moreover, there were at my table one hundred and fifty Jews and officials, besides those who came to us from the nations that were around us. 18 Now that which was prepared for each day was one ox and six choice sheep, also birds were prepared for me; and once in ten days all sorts of wine were furnished in abundance. Yet for all this I did not demand the governor's food allowance, because the servitude was heavy on this people.

Nehemiah could have used his position and power to his personal financial gain. He chose the path of servant leadership and put the welfare of the teams ahead of his own. This is leadership that is remembered with favor.

Further, the daily meal served as Nehemiah's communications touch point with all of the leadership of the project (i.e. the daily Scrum/Stand-up). If this was indeed how Nehehiah received information, reporting done in a relaxed setting, then this was an absolutely brilliant technique.

19 Remember me, O my God, for good, according to all that I have done for this people.

To be a good leader takes more than just having the right **Vision**, passion and **Drive** to get the job done. It takes a genuine care and respect for your teams backed up by a walk that walks the talk (and isn't just a bunch of empty checkmarks on a values poster sent to everyone on the teams from the internal marketing department).

The predecessor to the **4D Model** is the **4R Model**. To be a good leader, you must also understand the 4Rs when working with your team members at the personal level. The 4R's are as follows:

- **Right Ideas** (Truth, Doctrine, etc.)
- **Right Values & Attitudes**

- **Right Actions**
- **Right Results**

In addition to Luke 2:52, the **4R Model** is based on 2 Timothy 3,

> "All Scripture is inspired by God and profitable for teaching, for reproof, for correction, for training in righteousness; so that the man of God may be adequate, equipped for every good work."[39]

For us, this is the Right Truth. What is amazing to us is that there are a number of passages in the Bible that follow the **4R Model**. For example, in Joshua we read,

> "This book of the law shall not depart from your mouth (**Right Truth**), but you shall meditate on it day and night (**Right Values & Attitudes**), so that you may be careful to do according to all that is written in it (**Right Actions**); for then you will make your way prosperous, and then you will have success (**Right Results**)."[40]

1 Kings 2 follows a similar pattern,

> "Keep the charge of the Lord your God (**Right Truth**), to walk in His ways (**Right Values & Attitudes**), to keep His statutes, His commandments, His ordinances, and His

testimonies, according to what is written in the Law of Moses (**Right Actions**), that you may succeed in all that you do and wherever you turn (**Right Results**)."[41]

Another pattern prayer is recorded in the New Testament in Matthew 6 where Jesus taught us to,

"Pray, then, in this way: 'Our Father who is in heaven, Hallowed be Your name. Your kingdom come. Your will be done, On earth as it is in heaven (**Right Truth**). Give us this day our daily bread. And forgive us our debts, as we also have forgiven our debtors (**Right Values & Attitudes**). And do not lead us into temptation, but deliver us from evil (**Right Actions**). For Yours is the kingdom and the power and the glory forever (**Right Results**). Amen.'"[42]

At the individual level we show the **4R Model** as follows:

How is this useful to a project leader? Well, does it make sense that if you know each stakeholder's (including your team member's) "truth" and what they "value," then you can probably (within a range) predict their behavior ("actions"). If you can predict people's behavior, then you should be able to (again, within a range) predict the "results" that a stakeholder will produce. The **4R Model** works very effectively in reverse when a root-cause analysis is needed:

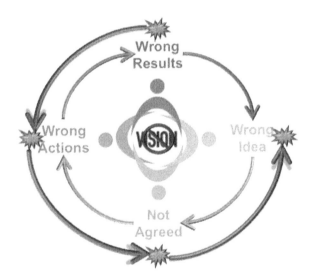

If you get the wrong results, it's probably due to someone doing the wrong thing. They most likely did the wrong thing because they were not in agreement with the original **Definition** (they had the wrong idea/truth).

Just like in the **4D Model**, the "**Vision**" for a person is tightly woven with the person's spirit as well. In the Christian view, a person is considered "spiritually" dead if they have not accepted Jesus Christ as personal Savior. A Christian should approach people management from a different perspective than a non-Christian.

Where this gets interesting is that even "secular," non-Church organizations recognize the need for understanding a person's spirit and their 'personal truth'. They approach it via character. For example, chapter 5 of the PMI code of ethics lays out the responsibility of each and every PMP to operate in a truthful (and honest) manner. The problem is that the "truth" can be mitigated or situationally **Defined** (as anyone that has ever studied marketing will point out). Our experience has been that the main way to know what a person has as their real truth is to observe their actions and results. Only then can you begin to determine the truth by which your team members actually live (walk vs. talk).

In our world of "situational" ethics (shades of gray, etc.), people can shift their "truth" on a daily basis (i.e. "...the situation has changed..." etc.). Even if you adhere to the idea of there being an absolute Truth (as we do), you still need to manage people at an individual level and manage him or her from their perspective of "truth" (understand and meet them where they're at, not necessarily where they should be by your **Definition**). Nehemiah spent this entire chapter on how to do this in the project setting.

The whole idea of having good **Definitions** ("truth") right up front in a project is to help eliminate (or at least mitigate) the "situation ethics" that will pop-up during a project.

The **4R Model** is the final link to cascading **Vision** down through the organization (we begin with using the **4D Model** from the organization level down to the project level and then at the personal level we use the **4R Model**):

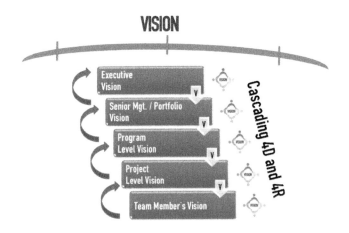

Organizations can cascade **Vision** a number of ways and can employ a number of governance models, but whatever methodology is used, the main goal is to move from abstract ideas to concrete actions that add value to the organization:

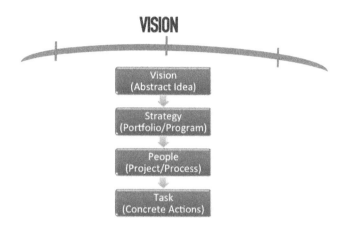

The main thing is to have a simple mechanism like "**VSPT**" inside your organization for quickly and accurately transmitting the **Vision**. An organization that can achieve that level of simplicity has just increased its odds of sustainability dramatically. This is why it is absolutely critical to have the right people on the bus (and the wrong people invited to find another bus).

Why is it so vital that people integrate **Vision** into their daily lives? There are a some key verses that support this foundational principal:

"For as he <u>thinks</u> within himself, so he is. He says to you, "Eat and drink!" But his heart is not with you."[43]

Our thought lives govern who we are. Any thought has the power to make or break us. Our hearts are the source of these thoughts. In Matthew

15:18-19, Jesus, the greatest servant leader that ever lived, taught us:

> "But the things that proceed out of the mouth come from the heart, and those defile the man. " For out of the heart come evil <u>thoughts</u>, murders, adulteries, fornications, thefts, false witness, slanders."[44]

And in Luke 6 he taught:

> "The good man out of the good treasure of his heart brings forth what is good; and the evil man out of the evil treasure brings forth what is evil; for his mouth speaks from that which fills his heart."[45]

James and John followed up on this idea in the following verses:

> "You lust and do not have; so you commit murder. You are envious and cannot obtain; so you fight and quarrel. You do not have because you do not ask."[46]

> "Everyone who hates his brother is a murderer; and you know that no murderer has eternal life abiding in him."[47]

What interesting is that it's not just the thoughts, but the passion involved with the thoughts. This is in line exactly with what Jesus taught:

"But I say to you that everyone who looks at a woman with lust for her has already committed adultery with her in his heart."[48]

It's a rather simple formula and it looks like this:

Thought (idea) + Passion +/- Ethics (good/ evil) = Potential Physical Equivalent

It is a foundational, Biblical Truth for all people that a thought that a person dwells on passionately will seek to manifest itself in the physical realm. Proverbs 4 says:

"Above all else, guard your heart, for everything you do flows from it."[49]

Even the tools of Greek Rhetoric echo this concept: Logos (Ideas) + Pathos (Passion) +/- Ethos (Ethics) = Rhema (Potential Physical Equivalent).

This is why **Vision** is so vital to your organization. It shapes the thoughts of your team member's hearts. Most organizations and organizations just don't seem to understand the power of this point. It is where true transformation takes place and is a massive game changer.

Vision is the key **Driver**.

Nehemiah Chapter 5 Action Steps

1. Do your team members see you leading from authority or power?

a. Do you act on the best interests of the team?
b. Do you ever try to cover for yourself at the expense of the team?
c. What changes could you make today to move away from power to authority?

2. Would your team members say you act with integrity if a blind survey were taken today?

a. What steps could you take today to begin walking with integrity?

3. Does your project and/or project team line up with the 4Rs?

a. If not, what steps do you need to take to correct this?

4. Are you getting the wrong results from your project?

a. Take a minute and use the **4R Model** to deconstruct the root cause.
b. Use that knowledge to craft a strategy to overcome this obstacle.

5. Do you know what your "truth" is and how it affects your team in both positive and negative ways?

a. Take a moment to ponder this question.

6. Do you have the right people on your project bus?

a. If you have square pegs working on a round peg project what steps can you take today to help those square pegs find their appropriate location in another project, and;

b. What will you do to find round pegs that meet your project needs?
7. Consider the impact of your thoughts on your project.
   a. Are your thoughts creating a postive or negative atmosphere?

Nehemiah 6

SISU (PASSIONATE PERSEVERANCE)

The word "Sisu" isn't in the English language. But it should be. It's a Finnish word that means "passionate perseverance," fortitude, guts, never-giving-up-no-matter-what-even-if-you-die … all of that in a single word. In the face of fierce opposition, Nehemiah exhibited wisdom, skill and Sisu:

> *1 Now when it was reported to Sanballat, Tobiah, to Geshem the Arab and to the rest of our enemies that I had rebuilt the wall, and that no breach remained in it, although at that time I had not set up the doors in the gates, 2 then Sanballat and Geshem sent a message to me, saying, "Come, let us meet together at Chephirim in the plain of Ono."*

Nehemiah had achieved **Drive (D4)** in verse 1! He and the teams had "rebuilt the wall and not a gap was left in it." But, even then, his enemies were trying to figure out how to derail the project. Risks still exist, even when a project is near completion. Project managers need to learn to recognize when a trap is being set. Nehemiah kept his focus:

> *But they were planning to harm me. 3 So I sent messengers to them, saying, "I am doing a great work and I cannot come down. Why should the work stop while I leave it and come down to you?" 4 They sent messages to me four times in this manner, and I answered them in the same way.*

Sanballat was persistent (like a bad cold he coming back over and over again), but Nehemiah persevered. Sanballat was even resorting to flights of fancy that rival any soap opera:

> *5 Then Sanballat sent his servant to me in the same manner a fifth time with an open letter in his hand. 6 In it was written, "It is reported among the nations, and Gashmu says, that you and the Jews are planning to rebel; therefore you are rebuilding the wall. And you are to be their king, according to these reports. 7 You have also appointed prophets to proclaim in Jerusalem concerning you, 'A king is in Judah!' And now it will be reported to the king according to these reports. So come now, let us take counsel together."*

Ever had an enemy lie about you, your team or your project? Sanballat was even using a powerful "sales" technique by trying to bring on a "witness." But Nehemiah saw through the ruse and recognized Sanballat's psychological warfare for what it really was, a very lame attempt at blackmail. I love Nehemiah's response:

> *8 Then I sent a message to him saying, "Such things as you are saying have not been done, but you are inventing them in your own mind."*

Wow. Nehemiah killed Sanballat's feeble attempt to blackmail them and he killed off the argument in a single, swift response. Nehemiah had total confidence in his executive sponsorship (the king and God) regardless of the external noise from Sanballat. Nehemiah clearly communicated to Sanballat that Sanballat had lost touch with reality and that his fantasy was going to get him into trouble.

But, Sanballat was employing a good military tactic – **fear**. Sanballat knew that if he could scare Nehemiah, the nobles and the teams, then he might have a shot at killing the project. Nehemiah knew that fear could destroy the project, too. But, Nehemiah exhibited, as he had throughout the project, servant leadership with an unwaivering focus on the **Vision**. This is now demonstrated at the **Driving** (**D4**) to success level:

> *9 For all of them were trying to frighten us, thinking, "They will become discouraged*

with the work and it will not be done." But now, O God, strengthen my hands.

Nehemiah responded correctly and prayed, wisely, for even more ability to passionately persevere. He prayed for Sisu! Nehemiah was confident that God would still provide the necessary strength to finish the project. Even then, the opposition was still rearing its ugly head:

10 When I entered the house of Shemaiah the son of Delaiah, son of Mehetabel, who was confined at home, he said, "Let us meet together in the house of God, within the temple, and let us close the doors of the temple, for they are coming to kill you, and they are coming to kill you at night."

Another trap was being set and Nehemiah smelled a rat. The enemy had paid-off one of the team members to spread fear from the inside:

11 But I said, "Should a man like me flee? And could one such as I go into the temple to save his life? I will not go in." 12 Then I perceived that surely God had not sent him, but he uttered his prophecy against me because Tobiah and Sanballat had hired him. 13 He was hired for this reason, that I might become frightened and act accordingly and sin, so that they might have an evil report in order that they could reproach me.

Sanballat was trying to find a way to cause Nehemiah to lose face. If Nehemiah had lost face, then the project even at this late stage would have been at risk. When all else failed, the project's enemy went after the integrity of the project manager. Sanballat was trying to re-define (a negative use of **Definitions** (**D1**) Nehemiah in order to disparage him.

If you want to spin a project off the table, throw the **Definitions** for the team into confusion. Remove the clarity and focus on **Vision**. This works most of the time. But, once again with continued focus on the **Vision**, we find Nehemiah still listening to God for direction and protection. Rather than confronting Sanballat and the other "antibodies" head-on, Nehemiah prayed:

14 Remember, O my God, Tobiah and Sanballat according to these works of theirs, and also Noadiah the prophetess and the rest of the prophets who were trying to frighten me.

15 So the wall was completed on the twenty-fifth of the month Elul, in fifty-two days. 16 When all our enemies heard of it, and all the nations surrounding us saw it, they lost their confidence; for they recognized that this work had been accomplished with the help of our God.

Transferring the project to their equivalent of "production, operations and support" didn't mean that Nehemiah's leadership headaches were over. Tobiah took over where Sanballat left off:

17 Also in those days many letters went from the nobles of Judah to Tobiah, and Tobiah's letters came to them. 18 For many in Judah were bound by oath to him because he was the son-in-law of Shecaniah the son of Arah, and his son Jehohanan had married the daughter of Meshullam the son of Berechiah. 19 Moreover, they were speaking about his good deeds in my presence and reported my words to him. Then Tobiah sent letters to frighten me.

Tobiah and Sanballat were sore losers. Nehemiah out-managed, out-performed and out-led them all. Tobiah and Sanballat clearly had aligned themselves to the wrong higher purpose and definitely didn't understand project or stakeholder management. Nehemiah, on the other hand, had reached the final milestone of the project and saw it through to a successful completion, elegantly navigating some very choppy political waters.

Nehemiah Chapter 6 Action Steps

1. Are you approaching your project with a "Sisu" attitude of passionate perseverance?
    a. If not, what would it take to move you to that level of commitment?
2. Have you considered the political risks that may exist as you come to the end of your project?
    a. What steps can you take to mitigate these late stage 'opportunities'?
    b. Have you considered not taking any action as the appropriate response?
3. What artifacts are you using to maintain continuous team and personal focus of the **Vision**?

RESOURCE MANAGEMENT

———

C hapter 7 of Nehemiah is a really the brief "closing report" for the project where we find Nehemiah turning the results of the project over to production, operations and support (i.e. the **gatekeepers**, the **singers**, the **Levites**, a **city manager** and a **military commander** for the citadel):

> *1 Now when the wall was rebuilt and I had set up the doors, and the gatekeepers and the singers and the Levites were appointed, 2 then I put Hanani my brother, and Hananiah the commander of the fortress, in charge of Jerusalem, for he was a faithful man and feared God more than many.*

Nehemiah put trusted and trustworthy leaders in charge of final details. But, you might ask, why appoint singers? The rest of the list makes sense, but singers? With the results that they had achieved, they really did have something about which to sing. It is important to acknowledge and celebrate you project's success so in this case, yes, singers. Nehemiah then gave them operational instructions:

> *3 Then I said to them, "Do not let the gates of Jerusalem be opened until the sun is hot, and while they are standing guard, let them shut and bolt the doors. Also appoint guards from the inhabitants of Jerusalem, each at his post, and each in front of his own house."*

In the "List of the Exiles Who Returned," we find that the walls have been rebuilt, but a city can't really function without people to inhabit it. In verse 5 we find that Nehemiah is still listening to God ("So my God put it into my heart…"). There is an aspect of listening and prayer in verse 5 that we just can't overlook if we want to be truly successful in whatever project God puts in our hearts. Nehemiah understood how to listen to the voice of God:

> *4 Now the city was large and spacious, but the people in it were few and the houses were not built. 5 Then my God put it into my heart to assemble the nobles, the officials and the people to be enrolled by genealogies. Then I found the book of the genealogy of those who came up first in which I found the following record: 6 These are the people of the province who came up from the captivity of the exiles whom Nebuchadnezzar the king of Babylon*

had carried away, and who returned to Jerusalem and Judah, each to his city, 7 who came with Zerubbabel, Jeshua, Nehemiah, Azariah, Raamiah, Nahamani, Mordecai, Bilshan, Mispereth, Bigvai, Nehum, Baanah. The number of men of the people of Israel: 8 the sons of Parosh, 2,172; 9 the sons of Shephatiah, 372; 10 the sons of Arah, 652; 11 the sons of Pahath-moab of the sons of Jeshua and Joab, 2,818; 12 the sons of Elam, 1,254; 13 the sons of Zattu, 845; 14 the sons of Zaccai, 760; 15 the sons of Binnui, 648; 16 the sons of Bebai, 628; 17 the sons of Azgad, 2,322; 18 the sons of Adonikam, 667; 19 the sons of Bigvai, 2,067; 20 the sons of Adin, 655; 21 the sons of Ater, of Hezekiah, 98; 22 the sons of Hashum, 328; 23 the sons of Bezai, 324; 24 the sons of Hariph, 112; 25 the sons of Gibeon, 95; 26 the men of Bethlehem and Netophah, 188; 27 the men of Anathoth, 128; 28 the men of Beth-azmaveth, 42; 29 the men of Kiriath-jearim, Chephirah and Beeroth, 743; 30 the men of Ramah and Geba, 621; 31 the men of Michmas, 122; 32 the men of Bethel and Ai, 123; 33 the men of the other Nebo, 52; 34 the sons of the other Elam, 1,254; 35 the sons of Harim, 320; 36 the men of Jericho, 345; 37 the sons of Lod, Hadid and Ono, 721; 38 the sons of Senaah, 3,930. 39 The priests: the sons of Jedaiah of the house of Jeshua, 973; 40 the sons of Immer, 1,052; 41 the sons of Pashhur,

*1,247; 42 the sons of Harim, 1,017.
43 The Levites: the sons of Jeshua, of Kadmiel,
of the sons of Hodevah, 74. 44 The singers:
the sons of Asaph, 148. 45 The gatekeepers:
the sons of Shallum, the sons of Ater, the
sons of Talmon, the sons of Akkub, the sons
of Hatita, the sons of Shobai, 138.*

*46 The temple servants: the sons of Ziha, the
sons of Hasupha, the sons of Tabbaoth, 47
the sons of Keros, the sons of Sia, the sons
of Padon, 48 the sons of Lebana, the sons of
Hagaba, the sons of Shalmai, 49 the sons of
Hanan, the sons of Giddel, the sons of Gahar,
50 the sons of Reaiah, the sons of Rezin,
the sons of Nekoda, 51 the sons of Gazzam,
the sons of Uzza, the sons of Paseah, 52 the
sons of Besai, the sons of Meunim, the sons
of Nephushesim, 53 the sons of Bakbuk,
the sons of Hakupha, the sons of Harhur,
54 the sons of Bazlith, the sons of Mehida,
the sons of Harsha, 55 the sons of Barkos,
the sons of Sisera, the sons of Temah, 56
the sons of Neziah, the sons of Hatipha.
57 The sons of Solomon's servants: the sons
of Sotai, the sons of Sophereth, the sons
of Perida, 58 the sons of Jaala, the sons of
Darkon, the sons of Giddel, 59 the sons of
Shephatiah, the sons of Hattil, the sons of
Pochereth-hazzebaim, the sons of Amon.
60 All the temple servants and the
sons of Solomon's servants were 392.*

61 These were they who came up from Tel-melah, Tel-harsha, Cherub, Addon and Immer; but they could not show their fathers' houses or their descendants, whether they were of Israel: 62 the sons of Delaiah, the sons of Tobiah, the sons of Nekoda, 642. 63 Of the priests: the sons of Hobaiah, the sons of Hakkoz, the sons of Barzillai, who took a wife of the daughters of Barzillai, the Gileadite, and was named after them. 64 These searched among their ancestral registration, but it could not be located; therefore they were considered unclean and excluded from the priesthood. 65 The governor said to them that they should not eat from the most holy things until a priest arose with Urim and Thummim.

The resources applied to this high-speed project were impressive:

66 The whole assembly together was 42,360, 67 besides their male and their female servants, of whom there were 7,337; and they had 245 male and female singers. 68 Their horses were 736; their mules, 245; 69 their camels, 435; their donkeys, 6,720.

Nehemiah organized just over **50,000 people** (49,942 listed above plus the 150 in Nehemiah's household for a total of 50,092 people to be exact) and **8,136 animals** (along with tons of wood, metal and stone blocks) from the lists above, into one of the **most astounding and remarkable agile projects** of all time:

- 150 leaders who came with Nehemiah from Babylon
- 42,360 inhabitants
- 7,337 menservants and maidservants
- 245 men and women singers
- 736 horses
- 245 mules
- 435 camels
- 6,720 donkeys

With these people, animals and resources at his disposal, Nehemiah and the teams rebuilt the walls of Jerusalem in **a mere 52 days**! If you are tasked with creating an agile organization with 50,000 team members, or more, then the principals outlined in this book give you the ancient wisdom and foundational truths that you will need to succeed at what was, until then, humanly impossible.

As with any good project, Nehemiah needed to manage, integrate and communicate the "triple constraints" (or competing demands) – Time, Cost and Scope along with quality, resources and risk in order to achieve a truly remarkable ROI (return on investment):

Project Triple Constraints

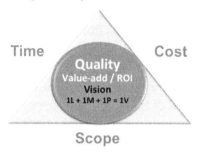

Any project manager or ScrumMaster will imme-diate recognize Figure 29. In traditional methodol-ogies it's call the "triple constraints." In Scrum it's called the Iron Triangle.

Thus far we had focused on:

- **People** (HR); **Procurements** (the wood, stones, mortar, metals parts, the animals and wagons to transport everything);
- **Scope** (the walls to full height with gates are bars in place);
- **Risk** (dealing with a credible external project enemy); and,
- **Time** (in an amazing 52 days!).

But, we've not really looked at what this project cost. While we don't have a full cost accounting provided to us by Nehemiah, here are some of the **monetary (Cost)** inputs to his amazing project:

*70 Some from among the heads of fathers'
households gave to the work. The governor
gave to the treasury 1,000 gold drachmas,
50 basins, 530 priests' garments. 71 Some
of the heads of fathers' households gave
into the treasury of the work 20,000 gold
drachmas and 2,200 silver minas. 72 That
which the rest of the people gave was 20,000
gold drachmas and 2,000 silver minas and 67
priests' garments.*

Here's the estimated monetary input that's been recorded for us (rounded to the nearest 100):

Who	What	Total
Governor	1000 D gold	$295,500
	50 Bowls	$7,500
	530 Garments	$530,000
Heads of Families	20,000 D gold	$5,832,200
	2,200 M silver	$678,700
Rest of the People	20,000 D gold	$5,832,200
	2,000 M silver	$622,200
	67 Garments	$67,000
	Total Budget:	$13,865,300

OK, so we don't use "drachmas" as currency today, but let's do some conversions, just to see what was input in today's approximate monetary value. The following were the rates of exchange at the time that this table was created:

- Gold was trading at 1.00 troy ounce = USD 1,296.04;

- Silver was trading at 1.00 troy ounce = USD 21.38;
- Let's assume $150 per bowl (doesn't say what they were made of, but we can assume they weren't cheap); and,
- Let's assume that the garments for the priests would have cost roughly the same as a better quality men's suit at a conservative estimate of USD 1,000 each.

Talk about having put your money where your mouth was! Almost $14 million in total cost for the project. This was no small budget for a group of refugees returning from captivity. This doesn't include the value of the input of the wood from the forests or the stones from the quarry.

When the project was completed, Nehemiah released the resources (the people, etc.) which still is a project management "best practice" even to this day; and, the people returned to their own hometowns. In a Scrum environment the team would stay together but they would be released for appointment to the next project as a team.

73 Now the priests, the Levites, the gate-keepers, the singers, some of the people, the temple servants and all Israel, lived in their cities. And when the seventh month came, the sons of Israel were in their cities.

There is another excellent verse on **Vision** from Habakkuk 2 that reads:

"Then the LORD answered me and said, 'Record the vision And inscribe it on tablets, That the one who reads it may run.'"[50]

Isn't that what any executive really wants? That the team understands the **Vision** and can run with it? But, in what was to become one of the first applications of an iterative principle that is found throughout God's word, Nehemiah understood that the iterative process needed to begin again when doing the transition from the project to production, operations and support.

What did he do? He went right back to **Definitions** (**D1**) in order to kick-off the transfer. Nehemiah instructed Ezra read the Law to the people after they had settled back into normal daily life in verse 73 above.

As we will see in the next chapter, the completion of the work takes us to the best part of any successful project: celebration!

Nehemiah Chapter 7 Action Steps

1. Do you have a simple framework that allows you to adapt and adjust to quickly changing circumstances while maintaining focus on the project and organizational **Vision**?
   a. Are your project finances understood well enough that you could execute a $14,000,000 project in 52 days?

2. How could you simplify the accounting to maximize the speed of **Delivery** for your project?
3. Do you plan and execute celebrations at the end of your projects?
    a. If not, why?
    b. Can you come up with creative ways to celebrate that do not increase project cost but recognize the effort of the team in **Delivering** a successful outcome?

REIGNITING THE VISION, THE LAW AND CELEBRATION!

---

1 And all the people gathered as one man at the square which was in front of the Water Gate, and they asked Ezra the scribe to bring the book of the law of Moses which the Lord had given to Israel.

The communication principles of this chapter are still "best practice" today. The **Definition (D1)**, i.e. the Law, was read out loud for everyone old enough to understand it. Remember the "mental" aspects of Luke 2:52? This is that verse in action.

2 Then Ezra the priest brought the law before the assembly of men, women and all who could listen with understanding, on the first day of the seventh month. 3 He read from it before the square which was in front of the Water Gate from early morning until midday,

*in the presence of men and women, those
who could understand; and all the people
were attentive to the book of the law.*

It's not just that the Law was read out loud, the
people actively listened. As they reflected on the
Law, it turned in to a rather solemn occasion.

*4 Ezra the scribe stood at a wooden podium
which they had made for the purpose. And
beside him stood Mattithiah, Shema, Anaiah,
Uriah, Hilkiah, and Maaseiah on his right
hand; and Pedaiah, Mishael, Malchijah,
Hashum, Hashbaddanah, Zechariah and
Meshullam on his left hand.*

When addressing large groups, make sure that
the speaker can be seen and heard by the audience.
This is group communications "101."

*5 Ezra opened the book in the sight of all
the people for he was standing above all
the people; and when he opened it, all the
people stood up. 6 Then Ezra blessed the Lord
the great God. And all the people answered,
"Amen, Amen!" while lifting up their hands;
then they bowed low and worshiped the Lord
with their faces to the ground.*

In praising God, to whom all glory should be
given, Nehemiah was, in a way, also thanking the
teams for their efforts. God's not necessarily going

to do for us that which we can do for ourselves. God will, however, provide the strength we need to complete the tasks at hand. That is really a tremendous promise.

The **Definition**, the Law, was read out loud and the people responded in Agreement (which is part of **D1** and **D2**).

> *7 Also Jeshua, Bani, Sherebiah, Jamin, Akkub, Shabbethai, Hodiah, Maaseiah, Kelita, Azariah, Jozabad, Hanan, Pelaiah, the Levites, explained the law to the people while the people remained in their place. 8 They read from the book, from the law of God, translating to give the sense so that they understood the reading.*

The Bible tells us that the Word of God is sharper than any double-edged sword, Nehemiah believed this and used the Bible as the artifact to **Drive (D4) Distilled Agreement (D2)** at a personal level.

Actually, what we see here is the **4R model** in operation. They were internalizing the **R1 – Right Truth** and realizing that they had previously had the **wrong values and attitudes**. Having the **Right Truth** enabled them to understand what the **R2 – Right Values and Attitudes** should have been. But their "walk" **R3 – Actions** hadn't matched the "talk." This grieved the people deeply:

> *9 Then Nehemiah, who was the governor, and Ezra the priest and scribe, and the*

Levites who taught the people said to all the people, "This day is holy to the Lord your God; do not mourn or weep." For all the people were weeping when they heard the words of the law.

Nehemiah understood that the "reset" button had just been pushed in the people's hearts. The "**Vision**" had just been transferred to production, operations and support.

He knew that with the remarkable results **R4** that they had just achieved, now was NOT the time for sorrow. It was time to celebrate the completion of the most successful Agile project of all time!

10 Then he said to them, "Go, eat of the fat, drink of the sweet, and send portions to him who has nothing prepared; for this day is holy to our Lord. Do not be grieved, for the joy of the Lord is your strength." 11 So the Levites calmed all the people, saying, "Be still, for the day is holy; do not be grieved."

The people's actions (**R3 – Right Actions**) were now correct because they now had a proper understanding of the Law.

12 All the people went away to eat, to drink, to send portions and to celebrate a great festival, because they understood the words which had been made known to them. 13 Then on the second day the heads of

*fathers' households of all the people, the
priests and the Levites were gathered to Ezra
the scribe that they might gain insight into
the words of the law. 14 They found written
in the law how the Lord had commanded
through Moses that the sons of Israel
should live in booths during the feast of the
seventh month. 15 So they proclaimed and
circulated a proclamation in all their cities
and in Jerusalem, saying, "Go out to the
hills, and bring olive branches and wild olive
branches, myrtle branches, palm branches
and branches of other leafy trees, to make
booths, as it is written."*

From a team building and community building
perspective, the order to celebrate by Nehemiah
was God-inspired genius. And the final results (**R4
– Right Results**) in verse 17 was unity. What a party!
What a celebration. What great joy!!! When we've
been successful with a project, it is essential for the
leadership to recognize the efforts of the team and
celebrate with them.

*16 So the people went out and brought them
and made booths for themselves, each on his
roof, and in their courts and in the courts of
the house of God, and in the square at the
Water Gate and in the square at the Gate
of Ephraim. 17 The entire assembly of those
who had returned from the captivity made
booths and lived in them. The sons of Israel*

had indeed not done so from the days of Joshua the son of Nun to that day. And there was great rejoicing.

If you just completed a $14 million project, with 50,000 people in 52 days, then you will definitely want to celebrate! You will have valid cause for one of the biggest celebrations of all time.

Nehemiah and Ezra continued to use the **4D and 4R Models** for the balance of the month after the walls had been completed. They made sure that there was enough time spent with production, operations and support to ensure that the "**Vision**" for the future was transferred to the teams.

18 He read from the book of the law of God daily, from the first day to the last day. And they celebrated the feast seven days, and on the eighth day there was a solemn assembly according to the ordinance.

It all begins and ends with having the proper Definitions.

A good portion of Servant leadership is making sure that your teams understand the **Definitions**, that they've internalized those **Definitions** and that they know how to live and walk the **Definitions** as they follow your example.

Nehemiah Chapter 8 Action Steps

1. Do you have celebrations as an action step in closing your projects or as a part of your final Sprint retrospective?
   a. If not, why?
2. The team in Nehemiah wanted more instruction related to the **Vision**. Is your team hungry to grow?
3. What are you doing to facilitate and accelerate this desire for growth?

NEHEMIAH 9

REFOCUSING THE TEAMS

1 Now on the twenty-fourth day of this month the sons of Israel assembled with fasting, in sackcloth and with dirt upon them. 2 The descendants of Israel separated themselves from all foreigners, and stood and confessed their sins and the iniquities of their fathers. 3 While they stood in their place, they read from the book of the law of the Lord their God for a fourth of the day; and for another fourth they confessed and worshiped the Lord their God. 4 Now on the Levites' platform stood Jeshua, Bani, Kadmiel, Shebaniah, Bunni, Sherebiah, Bani and Chenani, and they cried with a loud voice to the Lord their God. 5 Then the Levites, Jeshua, Kadmiel, Bani, Hashabneiah, Sherebiah, Hodiah, Shebaniah and Pethahiah, said, "Arise, bless the Lord your God forever and ever! O may Your glorious name be blessed And exalted above all blessing and praise!

6 *"You alone are the Lord.*
You have made the heavens,
The heaven of heavens with all their host,
The earth and all that is on it,
The seas and all that is in them.
You give life to all of them
And the heavenly host bows down before You.
7 *"You are the Lord God,*
Who chose Abram
And brought him out from Ur of the Chaldees,
And gave him the name Abraham.
8 *"You found his heart faithful before You,*
And made a covenant with him
To give him the land of the Canaanite,
Of the Hittite and the Amorite,
Of the Perizzite, the Jebusite and the Girgashite—
To give it to his descendants.
And You have fulfilled Your promise,
For You are righteous.
9 *"You saw the affliction of our fathers in Egypt,*
And heard their cry by the Red Sea.
10 *"Then You performed signs and wonders against Pharaoh, Against all his servants and all the people of his land; For You knew that they acted arrogantly toward them,*
And made a name for Yourself as it is this day.
11 *"You divided the sea before them, So they passed through the midst of the sea on dry ground;*
And their pursuers You hurled into the depths,
Like a stone into raging waters.

12 "And with a pillar of cloud You led them by day,
And with a pillar of fire by night
To light for them the way
In which they were to go.
13 "Then You came down on Mount Sinai,
And spoke with them from heaven;
You gave them just ordinances and true laws,
Good statutes and commandments.
14 "So You made known to them Your holy sabbath, And laid down for them command-ments, statutes and law,
Through Your servant Moses.
15 "You provided bread from heaven for them for their hunger, You brought forth water from a rock for them for their thirst,
And You told them to enter in order to possess The land which You swore to give them.

Verses 16 – 17 reinforce the enormous value of sharing the tribal stories (i.e. lessons learned). If we can't learn from the mistakes of the previous ScrumMasters and project leaders, then we will probably make the same mistakes ourselves. If we see the consequences of not aligning ourselves and our projects to the right higher purpose, of ignoring previous generations of leaders and their wisdom along with simply ignoring the past:

16 "But they, our fathers, acted arrogantly;
They became stubborn and would not listen to Your commandments.

17 "They refused to listen, And did not remember Your wondrous deeds which You had performed among them; So they became stubborn and appointed a leader to return to their slavery in Egypt.
But You are a God of forgiveness,
Gracious and compassionate,
Slow to anger and abounding in lovingkindness;
And You did not forsake them.
18 "Even when they made for themselves
A calf of molten metal
And said, 'This is your God
Who brought you up from Egypt,'
And committed great blasphemies,
19 You, in Your great compassion,
Did not forsake them in the wilderness;
The pillar of cloud did not leave them by day,
To guide them on their way,
Nor the pillar of fire by night, to light for them the way in which they were to go.
20 "You gave Your good Spirit to instruct them, Your manna You did not withhold from their mouth,
And You gave them water for their thirst.
21 "Indeed, forty years You provided for them in the wilderness and they were not in want; Their clothes did not wear out, nor did their feet swell.
22 "You also gave them kingdoms and peoples, And allotted them to them as a boundary. They took possession of the land of Sihon the king of Heshbon

And the land of Og the king of Bashan.
23 "You made their sons numerous as the stars of heaven,
And You brought them into the land
Which You had told their fathers to enter and possess.
24 "So their sons entered and possessed the land. And You subdued before them the inhabitants of the land, the Canaanites,
And You gave them into their hand, with their kings and the peoples of the land,
To do with them as they desired.
25 "They captured fortified cities and a fertile land.
They took possession of houses full of every good thing,
Hewn cisterns, vineyards, olive groves,
Fruit trees in abundance.
So they ate, were filled and grew fat,
And reveled in Your great goodness.
26 "But they became disobedient and rebelled against You,
And cast Your law behind their backs
And killed Your prophets who had admonished them
So that they might return to You,
And they committed great blasphemies.
27 "Therefore You delivered them into the hand of their oppressors who oppressed them,
But when they cried to You in the time of their distress,

You heard from heaven, and according to Your great compassion
You gave them deliverers who delivered them from the hand of their oppressors.
28 "But as soon as they had rest, they did evil again before You;
Therefore You abandoned them to the hand of their enemies, so that they ruled over them.
When they cried again to You, You heard from heaven,
And many times You rescued them according to Your compassion,
29 And admonished them in order to turn them back to Your law.
Yet they acted arrogantly and did not listen to Your commandments but sinned against Your ordinances,
By which if a man observes them he shall live.
And they turned a stubborn shoulder and stiffened their neck, and would not listen.
30 "However, You bore with them for many years,
And admonished them by Your Spirit through Your prophets,
Yet they would not give ear.
Therefore You gave them into the hand of the peoples of the lands.
31 "Nevertheless, in Your great compassion You did not make an end of them or forsake them,
For You are a gracious and compassionate God.

32 "Now therefore, our God, the great, the mighty, and the awesome God, who keeps covenant and lovingkindness,
Do not let all the hardship seem insignificant before You,
Which has come upon us, our kings, our princes, our priests, our prophets, our fathers and on all Your people,
From the days of the kings of Assyria to this day.
33 "However, You are just in all that has come upon us;
For You have dealt faithfully, but we have acted wickedly.
34 "For our kings, our leaders, our priests and our fathers have not kept Your law
Or paid attention to Your commandments and Your admonitions with which You have admonished them.
35 "But they, in their own kingdom,
With Your great goodness which You gave them,
With the broad and rich land which You set before them,
Did not serve You or turn from their evil deeds.

In verses 36 – 37 – Nehemiah lays out the **D1** and **D2** for the transition plan for next phase of the nation of repopulating the city. Nehemiah confronted the brutal facts but put the plan into motion for reforming the nation, even a nation that was in slavery to a foreign power (Babylon):

36 *"Behold, we are slaves today,*
And as to the land which You gave to our
fathers to eat of its fruit and its bounty,
Behold, we are slaves in it.
37 *"Its abundant produce is for the kings*
Whom You have set over us because
of our sins;
They also rule over our bodies
And over our cattle as they please,
So we are in great distress.
38 *"Now because of all this*
We are making an agreement in writing;
And on the sealed document are the names
of our leaders, our Levites and our priests."

Chapter 9 ends with a new agreement in writing: signed, sealed and **Delivered**.

Nehemiah Chapter 9 Action Steps

1. Do you have tribal success stories that can be used to motivate and challenge your team?
   a. If not, begin to look for and codify your stories so they can be used in the future?
2. Are there brutal facts related to your project that need to be confronted?
   a. Take some time to brainstorm appropriate responses to these facts.
3. Do you use signed documents to remind all of the Stakeholders that we, both the team and themselves, are 'all in'?

NEHEMIAH 10

DEALING WITH UNJUST LEADERS AND LEADERSHIP

———

I n chapters 10 and 13 of Nehemiah we again see **D3** and **D4** coming into play, completing the **D1** and **D2** in chapter 9. For example, in verse 1 of chapter 10, we see that Nehemiah is now Governor of Israel (in addition to still being the cupbearer for the king of Babylon). That's amazing. A **servant** (cupbearer) became the **leader** (the Governor). Many organizations completely miss the fact that a good Product Owner or project manager will posses **ALL** of the traits of a good CEO. In other words, each and every Product Owner or project manager should be viewing himself or herself as a **mini-CEO**, regardless of what level they are at in the organization:

> *1 Now on the sealed document were the names of: Nehemiah the governor, the son of Hacaliah, and Zedekiah, 2 Seraiah, Azariah, Jeremiah, 3 Pashhur, Amariah, Malchijah, 4 Hattush,*

Shebaniah, Malluch, 5 Harim, Meremoth, Obadiah, 6 Daniel, Ginnethon, Baruch, 7 Meshullam, Abijah, Mijamin, 8 Maaziah, Bilgai, Shemaiah. These were the priests. 9 And the Levites: Jeshua the son of Azaniah, Binnui of the sons of Henadad, Kadmiel; 10 also their brothers Shebaniah, Hodiah, Kelita, Pelaiah, Hanan, 11 Mica, Rehob, Hashabiah, 12 Zaccur, Sherebiah, Shebaniah, 13 Hodiah, Bani, Beninu. 14 The leaders of the people: Parosh, Pahath-moab, Elam, Zattu, Bani, 15 Bunni, Azgad, Bebai, 16 Adonijah, Bigvai, Adin, 17 Ater, Hezekiah, Azzur, 18 Hodiah, Hashum, Bezai, 19 Hariph, Anathoth, Nebai, 20 Magpiash, Meshullam, Hezir, 21 Meshezabel, Zadok, Jaddua, 22 Pelatiah, Hanan, Anaiah, 23 Hoshea, Hananiah, Hasshub, 24 Hallohesh, Pilha, Shobek, 25 Rehum, Hashabnah, Maaseiah, 26 Ahiah, Hanan, Anan, 27 Malluch, Harim, Baanah.

Organizations recognize the need to operate with honesty and integrity. For example, in the past, the Scrum Alliance Code of Ethics stated, "All Scrum Alliance members have an obligation to themselves and to Scrum Alliance to represent themselves truthfully, professionally and in a non-misleading manner. All Scrum Alliance members shall:

- Be honest and accurate in presenting qualifications and experience in all communications with others

- Provide accurate information in a highly visible and timely manner
- Not engage in or condone behavior that is designed to deceive others."

In a similar way the entire code of ethics and conduct for PMI (the Project Management Institute) reflect being people of integrity and honesty. A person is only as good as their word, and if their word isn't worth anything, then neither is the person. Don't just "talk the talk," you have to "walk the talk." Servant leadership begins with having integrity and good moral character. It begins with having the right **Definitions (D1)**.

Any of the Product Owners, ScrumMasters or project managers in your organization that are in the top 10% of all performers should be viewed as executive-caliber and treated as such. Organizations should carefully manage how they reward, motivate and groom their Product Owners, ScrumMasters and project managers for the next level of governance. Organizations that overlook, or downplay, the role of their project management leaders might miss grooming the **servant leader** that could take their organization to the next level. Organizations that are able to sustain their growth and market positions are the ones that are able to tap their project management skills and leverage the full potential of the top performers (the Product Owners, ScrumMasters and/or project managers that consistently achieve **D3** and **D4**).

28 Now the rest of the people, the priests, the Levites, the gatekeepers, the singers, the temple servants and all those who had separated themselves from the peoples of the lands to the law of God, their wives, their sons and their daughters, all those who had knowledge and understanding, 29 are joining with their kinsmen, their nobles, and are taking on themselves a curse and an oath to walk in God's law (R1), which was given through Moses, God's servant, and to keep and to observe all the commandments of God our Lord, and His ordinances and His statutes; 30 and that we will not give our daughters to the peoples of the land or take their daughters for our sons. 31 As for the peoples of the land who bring wares or any grain on the sabbath day to sell, we will not buy from them on the sabbath or a holy day; and we will forego the crops the seventh year and the exaction of every debt (R2).

32 We also placed ourselves under obligation to contribute yearly one third of a shekel for the service of the house of our God (R3): 33 for the showbread, for the continual grain offering, for the continual burnt offering, the sabbaths, the new moon, for the appointed times, for the holy things and for the sin offerings to make atonement for Israel, and all the work of the house of our God.

34 Likewise we cast lots for the supply of wood among the priests, the Levites and

the people so that they might bring it to the house of our God, according to our fathers' households, at fixed times annually, to burn on the altar of the Lord our God, as it is written in the law; 35 and that they might bring the first fruits of our ground and the first fruits of all the fruit of every tree to the house of the Lord annually, 36 and bring to the house of our God the firstborn of our sons and of our cattle, and the firstborn of our herds and our flocks as it is written in the law, for the priests who are ministering in the house of our God. 37 We will also bring the first of our dough, our contributions, the fruit of every tree, the new wine and the oil to the priests at the chambers of the house of our God, and the tithe of our ground to the Levites, for the Levites are they who receive the tithes in all the rural towns. 38 The priest, the son of Aaron, shall be with the Levites when the Levites receive tithes, and the Levites shall bring up the tenth of the tithes to the house of our God, to the chambers of the storehouse. 39 For the sons of Israel and the sons of Levi shall bring the contribution of the grain, the new wine and the oil to the chambers; there are the utensils of the sanctuary, the priests who are ministering, the gatekeepers and the singers. Thus we will not neglect the house of our God (R4).

In verses 28 – 37 of chapter 10 we once again see the **4R Model** in full swing. **Right Truth (R1)** → **Right Values and Attitudes (R2)** → **Right Actions (R3)** → **Right Results (R4)**.

Nehemiah Chapter 10 Action Steps

1. Do you approach your project as a mini-CEO?
    a. How would a CEO approach this project differently if she were leading it?
    b. What steps can you take today to move toward operating with this mindset?
    c. Do you see yourself as a mini-CEO?
2. How does your project line up with the 4Rs?
3. How do you line up with the 4Rs at a personal level?
    a. What are you doing today facilitate and accelerate your own growth and understanding in this area?

NEHEMIAH 11

THROWING THE DICE AND TREATING THE TEAMS FAIRLY

I n chapter 11 of Nehemiah we see the implementation of the transition plan and the residents are moved into the city. The transitional overlap between the project and final product, service or result looks something like this:

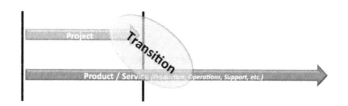

Nehemiah once again lists who settled in which part of the city. But it's interesting that only 10% of the team members were chosen to live in the city and that those 10% were literally chosen by "rolling the dice."

1 Now the leaders of the people lived in Jerusalem, but the rest of the people cast lots to bring one out of ten to live in Jerusalem, the holy city, while nine-tenths remained in the other cities.

Almost all of the project team members were clearly worthy of having the opportunity to live in the newly renovated city. Nehemiah solved a very sticky performance-reward issue by rolling the dice and allowing "random chance" (from a worldly perspective) to determine who got the reward. But, for believers it's evident that God's hand directed the roll of the dice.

The reaction of those not chosen to live in the city of Jerusalem in verse 2 communicated that the rest of the people commended those willing to live in the city, so it sort of sounds like it was the other 90% that were not chosen to live inside the walls of the city considered themselves the real winners in that raffle and were happy not to be chosen to live there:

2 And the people blessed all the men who volunteered to live in Jerusalem.
3 Now these are the heads of the provinces who lived in Jerusalem, but in the cities of Judah each lived on his own property in their cities—the Israelites, the priests, the Levites, the temple servants and the descendants of Solomon's servants. 4 Some of the sons of Judah and some of the sons of Benjamin lived

in Jerusalem. From the sons of Judah: Athaiah the son of Uzziah, the son of Zechariah, the son of Amariah, the son of Shephatiah, the son of Mahalalel, of the sons of Perez; 5 and Maaseiah the son of Baruch, the son of Col-hozeh, the son of Hazaiah, the son of Adaiah, the son of Joiarib, the son of Zechariah, the son of the Shilonite. 6 All the sons of Perez who lived in Jerusalem were 468 able men.

7 Now these are the sons of Benjamin: Sallu the son of Meshullam, the son of Joed, the son of Pedaiah, the son of Kolaiah, the son of Maaseiah, the son of Ithiel, the son of Jeshaiah; 8 and after him Gabbai and Sallai, 928. 9 Joel the son of Zichri was their over-seer, and Judah the son of Hassenuah was second in command of the city.

10 From the priests: Jedaiah the son of Joiarib, Jachin, 11 Seraiah the son of Hilkiah, the son of Meshullam, the son of Zadok, the son of Meraioth, the son of Ahitub, the leader of the house of God, 12 and their kinsmen who performed the work of the temple, 822; and Adaiah the son of Jeroham, the son of Pelaliah, the son of Amzi, the son of Zechariah, the son of Pashhur, the son of Malchijah, 13 and his kinsmen, heads of fathers' households, 242; and Amashsai the son of Azarel, the son of Ahzai, the son of Meshillemoth, the son of Immer, 14 and their brothers, valiant warriors, 128. And their overseer was Zabdiel, the son of Haggedolim.

15 Now from the Levites: Shemaiah the son of Hasshub, the son of Azrikam, the son of Hashabiah, the son of Bunni; 16 and Shabbethai and Jozabad, from the leaders of the Levites, who were in charge of the outside work of the house of God; 17 and Mattaniah the son of Mica, the son of Zabdi, the son of Asaph, who was the leader in beginning the thanksgiving at prayer, and Bakbukiah, the second among his brethren; and Abda the son of Shammua, the son of Galal, the son of Jeduthun. 18 All the Levites in the holy city were 284.

19 Also the gatekeepers, Akkub, Talmon and their brethren who kept watch at the gates, were 172.

20 The rest of Israel, of the priests and of the Levites, were in all the cities of Judah, each on his own inheritance. 21 But the temple servants were living in Ophel, and Ziha and Gishpa were in charge of the temple servants. 22 Now the overseer of the Levites in Jerusalem was Uzzi the son of Bani, the son of Hashabiah, the son of Mattaniah, the son of Mica, from the sons of Asaph, who were the singers for the service of the house of God. 23 For there was a commandment from the king concerning them and a firm regulation for the song leaders day by day. 24 Pethahiah the son of Meshezabel, of the sons of Zerah the son of Judah, was the king's representative in all matters concerning the people.

25 Now as for the villages with their fields, some of the sons of Judah lived in Kiriath-arba and its towns, in Dibon and its towns, and in Jekabzeel and its villages, 26 and in Jeshua, in Moladah and Beth-pelet, 27 and in Hazar-shual, in Beersheba and its towns, 28 and in Ziklag, in Meconah and in its towns, 29 and in En-rimmon, in Zorah and in Jarmuth, 30 Zanoah, Adullam, and their villages, Lachish and its fields, Azekah and its towns. So they encamped from Beersheba as far as the valley of Hinnom. 31 The sons of Benjamin also lived from Geba onward, at Michmash and Aija, at Bethel and its towns, 32 at Anathoth, Nob, Ananiah, 33 Hazor, Ramah, Gittaim, 34 Hadid, Zeboim, Neballat, 35 Lod and Ono, the valley of craftsmen. 36 From the Levites, some divisions in Judah belonged to Benjamin.

Nehemiah Chapter 11 Action Steps

1. Are you willing to take on a role or task that benefits the team even if it is not particularly in your best interest to accept that role or task?
2. How does this inform your path toward servant leadership?
3. What steps can you take today to move toward operating with a servant leaders mindset?

THE EXECUTIVE TEAM MEMBERS ACKNOWLEDGED

———

C hapter 12 is divided into 2 parts. In the first half, the priests and Levites are mentioned in verses 1 through 26 where Nehemiah is once again mentioned as the Governor and Ezra as a priest and scribe.

In the second half of the chapter, we see Nehemiah and the teams, once again, celebrating the victory of a major accomplishment. This party even outdid the first one. We see additional managers being appointed/promoted as part of the celebrations.

> *1 Now these are the priests and the Levites who came up with Zerubbabel the son of Shealtiel, and Jeshua: Seraiah, Jeremiah, Ezra, 2 Amariah, Malluch, Hattush, 3 Shecaniah, Rehum, Meremoth, 4 Iddo, Ginnethoi, Abijah, 5 Mijamin, Maadiah, Bilgah, 6 Shemaiah and*

Joiarib, Jedaiah, 7 Sallu, Amok, Hilkiah and Jedaiah. These were the heads of the priests and their kinsmen in the days of Jeshua.

8 The Levites were Jeshua, Binnui, Kadmiel, Sherebiah, Judah, and Mattaniah who was in charge of the songs of thanksgiving, he and his brothers. 9 Also Bakbukiah and Unni, their brothers, stood opposite them in their service divisions. 10 Jeshua became the father of Joiakim, and Joiakim became the father of Eliashib, and Eliashib became the father of Joiada, 11 and Joiada became the father of Jonathan, and Jonathan became the father of Jaddua.

12 Now in the days of Joiakim, the priests, the heads of fathers' households were: of Seraiah, Meraiah; of Jeremiah, Hananiah; 13 of Ezra, Meshullam; of Amariah, Jehohanan; 14 of Malluchi, Jonathan; of Shebaniah, Joseph; 15 of Harim, Adna; of Meraioth, Helkai; 16 of Iddo, Zechariah; of Ginnethon, Meshullam; 17 of Abijah, Zichri; of Miniamin, of Moadiah, Piltai; 18 of Bilgah, Shammua; of Shemaiah, Jehonathan; 19 of Joiarib, Mattenai; of Jedaiah, Uzzi; 20 of Sallai, Kallai; of Amok, Eber; 21 of Hilkiah, Hashabiah; of Jedaiah, Nethanel.

22 As for the Levites, the heads of fathers' households were registered in the days of Eliashib, Joiada, and Johanan and Jaddua; so were the priests in the reign of Darius the Persian. 23 The sons of Levi, the heads

of fathers' households, were registered in the Book of the Chronicles up to the days of Johanan the son of Eliashib. 24 The heads of the Levites were Hashabiah, Sherebiah and Jeshua the son of Kadmiel, with their brothers opposite them, to praise and give thanks, as prescribed by David the man of God, division corresponding to division. 25 Mattaniah, Bakbukiah, Obadiah, Meshullam, Talmon and Akkub were gatekeepers keeping watch at the storehouses of the gates. 26 These served in the days of Joiakim the son of Jeshua, the son of Jozadak, and in the days of Nehemiah the governor and of Ezra the priest and scribe.

27 Now at the dedication of the wall of Jerusalem they sought out the Levites from all their places, to bring them to Jerusalem so that they might celebrate the dedication with gladness, with hymns of thanksgiving and with songs to the accompaniment of cymbals, harps and lyres. 28 So the sons of the singers were assembled from the district around Jerusalem, and from the villages of the Netophathites, 29 from Beth-gilgal and from their fields in Geba and Azmaveth, for the singers had built themselves villages around Jerusalem. 30 The priests and the Levites purified themselves; they also purified the people, the gates and the wall.

31 Then I had the leaders of Judah come up on top of the wall, and I appointed two great choirs, the first proceeding to the right on top of the wall toward the Refuse Gate. 32 Hoshaiah and half of the leaders of Judah followed them, 33 with Azariah, Ezra, Meshullam, 34 Judah, Benjamin, Shemaiah, Jeremiah, 35 and some of the sons of the priests with trumpets; and Zechariah the son of Jonathan, the son of Shemaiah, the son of Mattaniah, the son of Micaiah, the son of Zaccur, the son of Asaph, 36 and his kinsmen, Shemaiah, Azarel, Milalai, Gilalai, Maai, Nethanel, Judah and Hanani, with the musical instruments of David the man of God. And Ezra the scribe went before them. 37 At the Fountain Gate they went directly up the steps of the city of David by the stairway of the wall above the house of David to the Water Gate on the east.

38 The second choir proceeded to the left, while I followed them with half of the people on the wall, above the Tower of Furnaces, to the Broad Wall, 39 and above the Gate of Ephraim, by the Old Gate, by the Fish Gate, the Tower of Hananel and the Tower of the Hundred, as far as the Sheep Gate; and they stopped at the Gate of the Guard. 40 Then the two choirs took their stand in the house of God. So did I and half of the officials with me; 41 and the priests, Eliakim, Maaseiah, Miniamin, Micaiah, Elioenai, Zechariah and Hananiah, with the trumpets; 42 and Maaseiah, Shemaiah, Eleazar, Uzzi, Jehohanan, Malchijah, Elam and

Ezer. And the singers sang, with Jezrahiah their leader, 43 and on that day they offered great sacrifices and rejoiced because God had given them great joy, even the women and children rejoiced, so that the joy of Jerusalem was heard from afar.

44 On that day men were also appointed over the chambers for the stores, the contributions, the first fruits and the tithes, to gather into them from the fields of the cities the portions required by the law for the priests and Levites; for Judah rejoiced over the priests and Levites who served. 45 For they performed the worship of their God and the service of purification, together with the singers and the gatekeepers in accordance with the command of David and of his son Solomon. 46 For in the days of David and Asaph, in ancient times, there were leaders of the singers, songs of praise and hymns of thanksgiving to God. 47 So all Israel in the days of Zerubbabel and Nehemiah gave the portions due the singers and the gatekeepers as each day required, and set apart the consecrated portion for the Levites, and the Levites set apart the consecrated portion for the sons of Aaron.

Nehemiah Chapter 12 Action Steps

1. Are you looking for leaders based on their abilities and **Delivery** skills on a project?
   a. If not, why?

    b. What do you base your decisions on?

2. Do you make plans for specific, continuous celebrations for your teams?

3. If not, what can you do today to begin celebrating success on a regular basis?

NEHEMIAH 13

POST PROJECT SUPPORT AND LEADERSHIP

———

I n chapter 13, we see that once again things are
capable of spinning off the table during the transition phase. While the cat's away, the mice will play.
When there is a vacuum of leadership, it seems that
people will try to take advantage of the situation. In
verses 1 through 14 we find that Eliashib was exactly
that type of character.

Verse 10 highlights that even a good plan with
good leaders can go sideways during the production,
operations and support phase if there is not proper
oversight and attention to **Delivery** (**D4**).

*1 On that day they read aloud from the
book of Moses in the hearing of the people;
and there was found written in it that no
Ammonite or Moabite should ever enter the
assembly of God, 2 because they did not meet
the sons of Israel with bread and water, but*

hired Balaam against them to curse them. However, our God turned the curse into a blessing. 3 So when they heard the law, they excluded all foreigners from Israel.

4 Now prior to this, Eliashib the priest, who was appointed over the chambers of the house of our God, being related to Tobiah, 5 had prepared a large room for him, where formerly they put the grain offerings, the frankincense, the utensils and the tithes of grain, wine and oil prescribed for the Levites, the singers and the gatekeepers, and the contributions for the priests. 6 But during all this time I was not in Jerusalem, for in the thirty-second year of Artaxerxes king of Babylon I had gone to the king. After some time, however, I asked leave from the king, 7 and I came to Jerusalem and learned about the evil that Eliashib had done for Tobiah, by preparing a room for him in the courts of the house of God. 8 It was very displeasing to me, so I threw all of Tobiah's household goods out of the room. 9 Then I gave an order and they cleansed the rooms; and I returned there the utensils of the house of God with the grain offerings and the frankincense.

10 I also discovered that the portions of the Levites had not been given them, so that the Levites and the singers who performed the service had gone away, each to his own field (D4). 11 So I reprimanded the officials and said, "Why is the house of God forsaken?"

Then I gathered them together and restored them to their posts. 12 All Judah then brought the tithe of the grain, wine and oil into the storehouses.

But, once Nehemiah returned to Jerusalem, in verse 13 he put things back in order and appointed three trustworthy and reliable team members (Shelemiah, Zadok and Pedaiah) applying **VSPT** along with an assistant (Hanan). By appointing two, Nehemiah had put in place a check and balance.

13 In charge of the storehouses I appointed Shelemiah the priest, Zadok the scribe, and Pedaiah of the Levites, and in addition to them was Hanan the son of Zaccur, the son of Mattaniah; for they were considered reliable, and it was their task to distribute to their kinsmen. 14 Remember me for this, O my God, and do not blot out my loyal deeds which I have performed for the house of my God and its services.

Nehemiah recounts for us in verses 15 through 22 how it didn't take long for the team members to deviate from the **Vision** to which they had agreed (back in the end of chapter 9 and beginning of chapter 10) and even put their signatures and seals to that agreement. They were doing business on the Sabbath, which was clearly not in alignment with the agreed to **Definitions** (**D1** and **D2**).

In order to protect the **Vision**, Nehemiah went as far as to enforce the **Vision** using military might (he stationed guards and threatened them with physical violence if they kept misbehaving).

Even though we aren't necessarily able to use the threat of physical violence today, every Product Owner, ScrumMaster and project manager will be faced at some point in their career with the fact that sometimes the threat of force or actual force (i.e. loss of job, demotion, etc.) is needed to maintain alignment with the organization's core values and **Vision**.

> *15 In those days I saw in Judah some who were treading wine presses on the sabbath, and bringing in sacks of grain and loading them on donkeys, as well as wine, grapes, figs and all kinds of loads, and they brought them into Jerusalem on the sabbath day. So I admonished them on the day they sold food. 16 Also men of Tyre were living there who imported fish and all kinds of merchandise, and sold them to the sons of Judah on the sabbath, even in Jerusalem. 17 Then I reprimanded the nobles of Judah and said to them, "What is this evil thing you are doing, by profaning the sabbath day? 18 Did not your fathers do the same, so that our God brought on us and on this city all this trouble? Yet you are adding to the wrath on Israel by profaning the sabbath."*

19 It came about that just as it grew dark at the gates of Jerusalem before the sabbath, I commanded that the doors should be shut and that they should not open them until after the sabbath. Then I stationed some of my servants at the gates so that no load would enter on the sabbath day. 20 Once or twice the traders and merchants of every kind of merchandise spent the night outside Jerusalem. 21 Then I warned them and said to them, "Why do you spend the night in front of the wall? If you do so again, I will use force against you." From that time on they did not come on the sabbath.

Sometimes people don't think that "no" actually means "no." The **greatest Servant Leader** of all time, **Jesus of Nazareth**, had this to say in Matthew 5 about people that have trouble with the concept of transparency:

"Simply let your **'Yes'** be 'Yes,' and your **'No**,' 'No'; **anything beyond this comes from the evil one**."[51]

The Apostle Paul had clearly run into the same kind of people along the way as well as recorded in 2 Corinthians 1:

"When I planned this, did I do it lightly? Or **do I make my plans in a worldly manner so**

that in the same breath I say, "Yes, yes" and "No, no"?"[52]

People who are able to say "yes" and "no" in the same breath are written about by James, the brother of Jesus, in James 1 that:

"He is a double-minded man, unstable in all he does."[53]

Have the guts (Sisu) and integrity to learn to be able to say yes or no and stick with it. Don't make promises that you can't (or won't) keep. It's actually better to say nothing than to make a promise that is unachievable. People of character learn to make promises only when they are absolutely sure that they can keep their promises. It's a key part of being truly transparent. This is a very tough standard for people to live up to in today's world but the resulting unleashed power of team unity and trust is worth the effort.

22 And I commanded the Levites that they should purify themselves and come as gatekeepers to sanctify the sabbath day. For this also remember me, O my God, and have compassion on me according to the greatness of Your lovingkindness.
23 In those days I also saw that the Jews had married women from Ashdod, Ammon and Moab. 24 As for their children, half spoke in the language of Ashdod, and none of them

*was able to speak the language of Judah, but
the language of his own people. 25 So I contended with them and cursed them and struck
some of them and pulled out their hair, and
made them swear by God, "You shall not give
your daughters to their sons, nor take of their
daughters for your sons or for yourselves. 26
Did not Solomon king of Israel sin regarding
these things? Yet among the many nations
there was no king like him, and he was loved
by his God, and God made him king over
all Israel; nevertheless the foreign women
caused even him to sin. 27 Do we then hear
about you that you have committed all this
great evil by acting unfaithfully against our
God by marrying foreign women?"*

Eliashib lost his position and was fired in verse
28 since he was allied with Sanballat (Nehemiah's
enemy) and because he had redefined his priestly
role in such a way that it was not in alignment with
the overall **Vision**:

*28 Even one of the sons of Joiada, the son of
Eliashib the high priest, was a son-in-law of
Sanballat the Horonite, so I drove him away
from me. 29 Remember them, O my God,
because they have defiled the priesthood
and the covenant of the priesthood and
the Levites.*
*30 Thus I purified them from everything
foreign and appointed duties for the priests*

and the Levites, each in his task, 31 and I arranged for the supply of wood at appointed times and for the first fruits. Remember me, O my God, for good.

Consideration of ongoing leadership development is a core part of every leaders ongoing responisibiltiy. Make sure you are raising up leaders as you bring your project to successful conclusion.

Nehemiah Chapter 13 Action Steps

1. Do you stay in touch with people in the production environment once your project result has been handed over?
    a. If not, why?
    b. Do you have quality check points at six month or twelve month intervals to validate realized benefits?
    c. Would this type of review strengthen your organization?
    d. Are there steps you can take to insure the lasting value your project was created to **Deliver** was indeed ongoing in its value?
2. Are you a transparent leader?
    a. Is this how your team would describe you in a blind survey?
    b. If not, what steps can you take today to become more transparent?

3. Are you willing to make tough, potentially unpopular decisions to maintain the **Delivery** of the project **Vision**?
   a. If not, why?
   b. What will it take for your own Sisu to rise up?
4. Are your communications clear?
   a. Is your 'yes' yes and your 'no' no?
   b. If not, find a mentor or a peer who will hold you accountable and help you grow in this area. It is important.
5. Are you planning and executing leadership development with your team members?
   a. What can you do today to begin or enhance your leadership development activities?

Nehemiah Section 3 Action Steps

1. Take some time to reflect on how these ancient principles **Delivered** such amazing results.
2. Write down the specific items that made sense and that can be immediately applied to your current projects.

SECTION 4 –
ENTERPRISE AGILE –
USING THE UVF AT THE PROGRAM MANAGEMENT OFFICE (PMO) LEVEL AND ABOVE TO SCALE TO 50K AND MORE

CHAPTER 6

GAINING A BUSINESS AGILE MINDSET AND AGILE PMO METHODOLOGY

Overview

"72% of all Apple revenue in 2011 was generated by the iPhone and iPad which did not exist as products five years ago." Nick Wingfield from the New York Times in an article published on January 25, 2012

Why is Agile such a hot topic now in project management circles? Because of the promise of speed and creating a culture that can adapt quickly to changing conditions.

The above quote is one small example of this reality because Apple is now the largest corporation in the world based upon capitalized value and its largest revenue stream is based on products that were only a concept just a few years ago. Companies must find new and better ways to respond and move based upon market changes and opportunities. Guy Kawasaki, who led marketing at Apple during the creation of the Macintosh Computer and who wrote *"The Art of the Start"* on page 13 stated it this way, "In these times, traditional market research is useless – there is no survey or focus group that can predict customer acceptance for a product or a service that you may barely be able to describe ... The wisest course of action is to take your best shot with a prototype, immediately get it to market, and iterate quickly.

If you wait for ideal circumstances in which you have all the information you need (which is impossible), the market will pass you by." We believe this is the reason Agile is rising in focus and attention within traditional corporate settings. Whatever 'it' is, we need it fast, we need it good and we need it to cost less. Got it?

Most situations that we have found across the world that describe themselves as 'agile', and we have been intricately involved in many, are really a blended mix of agile methodologies and traditional management structures. This should come as no surprise but it is important from a PMO point of view to understand because this blending will be true inside your organization as well. You will need to structure the PMO to take this into consideration. We will demonstrate in this chapter how you can easily accomplish this by using simple tools and frameworks to facilitate, communicate and report across these diverse styles and methods. Section 4 of this book **Defines** the Program level roles, ceremonies, artifacts, resource management and reporting necessary to adapt an organization's Program Management to accommodate a shift to Agile methodologies or when Agile methodologies are being added as an additional tool within a traditional PMO structure.

Scrum is the most common Agile methodology and, as we mentioned earlier, Scrum and Agile has been used interchangeably throughout this book and will be in this section as well. When we refer to "*Business Agile*," we are referring to the **UVF**, our proprietary business leadership framework.

In traditional business management the metaphor of Ready, Aim, Fire is usually flipped around to point out when a process is broken, for example, Ready, Fire, Aim. This is done to try to describe the irony of not taking time to aim and just firing blindly and thus reducing your chances for success.

Agile actually uses fire/adjust, fire/adjust, fire/adjust, fire/adjust as the standard and preferred approach to management.

Facebook as a company did not exist eight years ago and Dustin Moskovitz, Co-Founder of Facebook said, "work is about managing tasks, and responding to things quickly." But in a world where doing more with less and doing it faster is the mantra and being lean and agile the new normal we need processes and structures that allow us to fire/adjust, fire/

adjust, fire/adjust, fire/adjust until we arrive at sound results that **Deliver** value based upon the **Vision**.

We always strive for clear **Definitions**, including the **Vision** for what a preferred end state will be, prior to following a fire/adjust path. But more and more, the speed with which change is occurring **Drives** decisions and compresses time frames. Organizations must find new and better ways to respond and move based upon market changes and opportunities. We have found that our framework helps accomplish that end.

For a PMO to succeed, they need to do the following five items:

1. Focus on **Vision**
2. Have clear **Definitions**
3. **Distill** clear **Agreements**
4. Have clear, short plans and time frames for **Delivery**
5. **Drive** success with frequent communication and iterative continuous focus on **Vision** for decision making or change management

Of these five, **Vision** is the most important because if you are not governed by **Vision**, you will be **Driven** by circumstances. In other words, a business agile framework that **Defines**, collects, shares and adapts to fast changing environments based upon the unchanging **Vision** of the organization. Where this has been applied we have seen exponential results.

In setting up a PMO, we recommend using the **4D Model** from the **UVF** as shown in the previous **4D Model** Figures from Chapter 1 forward.

Chapter 6 Action Steps

1. Does your organization have a PMO or ePMO (Enterprise PMO)?
   a. If so, is it at the right level in the organization (i.e. does it report to an Executive level like the CTO, CIO or CSO 'Chief Strategy Officer')?
   b. If not, why not?
   c. What steps could you take today to improve project prioritization and tool standardization in the face of this lack?
2. Do you have an Enterprise framework that allows **Vision** to be reflected in the task level decisions?
3. Write down the **Vision** for the Program and Portfolio levels in your organization.
   a. Describe the links between the various cascading **Visions**, including your own personal **Vision** and how they link back to the level above it.
4. What are the Strategies for the Program and Portfolio levels?
   a. How are you linking your tasks to accomplish these Strategies?
   b. How are you communicating this to the appropriate Stakeholders?

CHAPTER 7

METHODOLOGY AGNOSTIC PROGRAM MANAGEMENT (4Ds)

One of the keys to success for an organization's Program Management is that whatever structure is chosen to manage the portfolio it needs to be a pragmatic approach. Each and every project in each program or portfolio should be linked to the overall organizational **Vision** (Portfolio level) and at least one of the key Strategies (Program Level) for the organization.

As we shared in Chapter 5, if your organization doesn't explicitly state a strategy, then a Project Manager, Product Owner and/or Program Manager can substitute one of the following three purposes for the project instead:

1. Increase Revenue
2. Reduce costs.
3. Eliminate or mitigate risk.

These are the three primary measurable reasons that an organization should ever do a project. The

UVF's Portfolio and Program management is a very simple model and its project, program and portfolio view looks like the following diagram:

Link Every Project to Vision and Strategy

A major exercise should be conducted by the PMO to help the leaders in charge of Programs and Portfolios align the bandwidth available for each of their teams with the projects that each leader deems as adding the most value to the organization, based upon the stated **Vision** for the organization.

For one company with which we worked, this involved reducing the Prioritized Project Backlog from over 250 projects to under 100 projects. This resulted in the Portfolio leader's aspirations being aligned with organizational capabilities and current state of being able to truly **Deliver** 70 projects +/- per year.

Later, the same company was able to almost double the throughput and was on target to

Deliver 120+ projects per year with the same level of resources. That exercise alone was worth hundreds of thousands of dollars in cost avoidance to the company in that they were able to reduce the size of their portfolios which reduced the internal, cross-functional "noise" level to almost zero.

In the sample reports in Chapter 9 of this book, the upper limit included in the graph is the number of projects agreed to by each of the Program and Portfolio leaders of this particular company for their prioritized list of projects for 2012. Since the leaders had a prioritized project backlog **Defined** for 2012, it was the assumption of the PMO that these projects represent the highest value features that would add the most value to the organization during that 12 month cycle. We have seen traditional portfolio management forecasting structures use unnecessarily complex financial formulas to rank or rate the value-added for each project. We have found that the Product Owners (and the Executive teams that they report to) are best able to rank and rate the highest value projects.

The organization in the case described above will have a mix of both Agile and Traditional projects for the foreseeable future. To move any organization from traditional to Business Agile thinking (in coordination with some type of "Agile Transition Team") will be, at minimum, a multi-year process. This is partly due to the fact that it will take time for an organization to mature in its usage of Agile project methodologies. It requires a high level of commitment from senior management and executive management to make the transition possible.

If there is not across-the-board support for the move, then the road to transition is a very long and risky one. This is especially true in companies that have a legacy of command-and-control organizational structures. However, Business Agile principles, applied correctly, will have immediate and positive impacts even on traditional PMOs and projects.

Program Charter – Definition (D1)

One you have the commitment and support of senior and executive management, you can then organize your Programs and Portfolios using the **4D Model** from the **UVF**. As we mentioned in our chapter on **Vision**, your **Definitions** for a Program Charter should include:

- The **VSPT** (links to **Vision**, Strategy for the Project and Tasks at hand)
- The **Definitions** for who, what, when, where, why and how:
  - Who (should be on the team)?
    - ◆ Resource Allocations
    - ◆ Time box during which resources are allocated (this is slightly different than the traditional view of "duration")
  - What (product, service, result)?
  - When (will we start)?
  - Where (co-located, multiple locations)?

- ◆ Keep in mind that organizational distance in the chart may be of greater significance that actual distance between the team members
- ○ Why (are we doing this project)?
  - ◆ Increase Revenues?
  - ◆ Decrease Costs?
  - ◆ Mitigate or eliminate Risk?
  - ◆ How (Traditional, Lean, Agile or Blended)?

This becomes the guiding road map for your program.

Defining Program Level Roles – Definition (D1)

As we shared in Chapter two, at the project level Scrum only recognizes the following roles:

- Product Owner
- ScrumMaster
- Developer

All other roles are "stakeholder" roles that are external to the team. The traditional Project Manager role has been dispersed among these three roles in Scrum.

Blended organizations will many times opt to use project managers for organizational management, program management and for reporting purposes. An organization may choose to have Program

Managers and perhaps even a Portfolio Manager or Director as needed.

The challenge for Project, Program and Portfolio Managers is that most organizations will end up using an undefined or ill-defined "Agile" Program Management approach that results in organizational dissonance.

The key here is that your PMO level leadership and Program Management structure are practical and simple so that as a PMO you can create a unified language across diverse functions and project types as shown below:

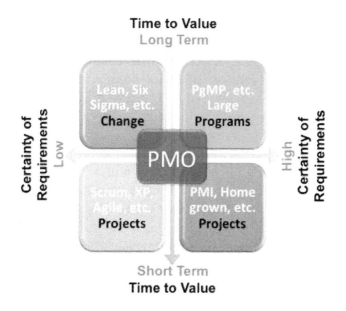

The role of the Project Manager and/or Program Manager will still be needed in most companies because they will be using multiple project management methodologies, reporting tools and frameworks ranging from traditional/waterfall to theories of constraints/lean to Agile/Scrum.

Project Managers and/or Program Managers will be responsible for guiding and reporting on all of the projects (both traditional and Agile) in their respective portfolios using the methodology as suggested in the chapter on reporting.

In a pure Scrum environment, the Project Manager's and/or Program Manager's role is more akin with that of a Product Owner. They will coordinate multiple Product Backlogs along with the dependencies and integration items that arise between the projects. Hopefully your Project Managers and/or Program Managers will have the depth of Agile experience to be able to do so. In that case, as long as they have domain expertise, it might make sense for your Project Managers and/or Program Managers to function as Product Owners instead of only being facilitators (i.e. ScrumMasters). This assumes that a Project Manager and/or Program Manager has both the training and a certification at the level of the CSPO or CSM (Certified Product Owner or ScrumMaster) along with at least a couple of years of hands-on experience using Agile/Scrum in projects. And as more companies attempt to integrate Scrum into traditional project management, what we have found is that these roles become more and more diluted and less and less pure Scrum.

Some Project Managers make very good ScrumMasters due to excellent facilitation skills.

Other Project Managers make very good Product Owners and/or Program Managers due to the depth of their domain experience. When transitioning to Agile, it is important for the organization to evaluate each Project Manager on a case-by-case basis to determine where they will best fit in the new organizational structure.

The long-term aspirational goals may be for the teams, along with the ScrumMaster and Product Owner, to eventually take over the Program Manager role as the organization becomes more mature in using the Scrum project management methodology. Over time the PMO has the expectation that the ScrumMasters and Product Owners will eventually be responsible for additional Program level meetings and be able to step into that role.

Scrum of Scrums is a specific project and program management tool for use with Scrum-based projects. At the beginning phase of an Agile transformation, many organizations will not be using the Scrum of Scrums. This is usually the case since almost every Scrum reference book suggests starting small and growing Scrum organically based on initial team successes. But, if an organization is going to opt to use Scrum of Scrums and can go with a purely Agile PMO implementation right from the start, then they might have the opportunity to substitute Product Owners for Program Managers.

The Scrum of Scrums is a meeting that usually includes the Product Owners from each of the multiple project teams that are working on the same Product to align those projects with each other using the Scrum of Scrums. Usually one Scrum Master from one of the project teams facilitates the Scrum of Scrums (the ScrumMasters from each project take turns leading the Scrum of Scrums) and the teams send a representative to the Scrum of Scrums depending upon the topic for that day. The questions asked and answered at the Scrum of Scrums are very similar to the ones asked in the daily Scrum, but at a higher level and will deal with cross dependencies and integration backlog items.

For teams using the Scrum of Scrums, we would encourage the reader to follow the recommendations from the Scrum Alliance for doing the Scrum of Scrums:

- "The Scrum of Scrum meetings occur daily
- If meeting daily, the following set of questions should be used:
    1. What did you do yesterday?
    2. What will you do today
    3. What obstacles are in your way or slowing you down?
- If meeting less often than daily, then the following set of questions should be used:
    What has your team done since we last met?
    What will your team do before we meet again?
    Is anything slowing your team down or getting in their way?
    Are you about to put something in another team's way?"[54]

The Scrum of Scrums is a mirror image of the daily Scrum meeting at the project level and can be used at either the project or program levels. It is essential that the team members participating in the Scrum of Scrums maintain the meeting discipline required for this to be successful. Blockers will be addressed after the meeting is finished. In addressing blockers, the main goal is to **Distill Agreement** on how to resolve and remove those obstacles.

Some organizations use a Scrum of Scrum of Scrums for Portfolio level meetings. Executive management in some organizations can facilitate this and in others it will be the role of the Portfolio Manager to do so. This meeting addresses exceptions and resource contentions between the Program and Portfolio leaders and helps remove blockers, impediments and obstacles for the Programs and Projects.

Program Level Ceremonies – Distilling Agreement (D2)

At all costs, we must resist the urge to return to comfort zones and over-complicate the Program Management of Agile/Scrum. Scrum is deceptively simple ... and definitely not easy. It requires a very high level of personal and team discipline to effectively use this methodology to its full potential. It's always best to keep it simple. Mike Beetle, one of the signers of the Agile Manifesto, stated during a Scrum training session in January 2012 that "Simplicity is the art of maximizing the amount of work not done", which was one of the original 'values' of Scrum. Jim Collins, on page 97 of "How the Mighty Fall" stated the same thought but from the Business perspective that "If you want to reverse decline, be rigorous about what not to do."

We would add to this that since Scrum teams are supposed to be self-organizing and self-governing that this does not happen without the individual team members being self-managed and self-motivated people. Jim Collins, on page 56 of "How the Mighty Fall" hit the nail on the head when he asserted "Any exceptional enterprise depends first and foremost upon having self-managed and self-motivated people – the #1 ingredient for a culture of discipline." Great Agile teams need leadership and motivated members to succeed. It is not merely a matter of waving a consultants handbook over a group of people and declaring them Agile because they attended a half-day seminar or a two-day certification course. It is a long, hard journey.

Each Program should be required to group its Products in associated Programs and then to break those down into multiple projects. Programs that have Agile/Scrum projects that are interdependent or require a high level of integration will need to be managed carefully.

Scaling Scrum is one of the most challenging parts of transitioning to Agile from traditional methodologies. To help group the projects, from a Program Level it can make sense to align projects by products. For example, for new product development the product/project team allocations might look something like this:

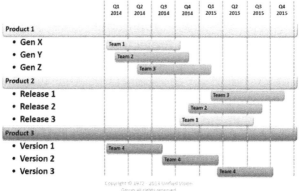

This way Programs can be organized in such a way as to help make sure that teams working on similar functionality and features can be integrated across multiple Products. For example, projects that are part of Product 1 above would then have a Program-level meeting (or Scrum of Scrums if used) to insure integration issues and dependencies are properly addressed.

Word of caution: Misunderstanding or misusing a chart like this could lead to meeting overload, both for the daily Scrum as well as the Scrum of Scrums. At all costs, Scrum of Scrums should be used carefully or else there is the risk that your teams will spend too much time attending meetings as compared to actually getting the work done. This again requires a high level of discipline, focus and crowd control.

If a blended approach is used, then the Program Managers will be using a more traditional Program

Management weekly or bi-weekly meeting to manage the Agile projects in their portfolios. Those meetings should be conducted and governed in a way that does not disturb the project level Scrum processes. Top-down approaches like Prince2, Managing Successful Projects (MSP), etc. do not work well with teams that are truly Agile. Therefore the PMO should set the expectation that Programs using those methodologies should adapt to Scrum as outlined in this chapter and in the Agile training materials used by their company. Failure to do so could result in a heavy command-and-control approach, choking the life out of Scrum projects at the team level.

The best way that we've found to mitigate the issues created when trying to use a matrix like the one above is to view all Business Agile Program Management (including Scrum) like a stadium:

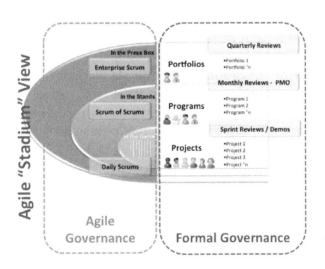

It really depends on the organization how much parallel governance that they want between traditional and Business Agile methodologies. If you are using the Scrum of Scrums, you can still use the Bi-weekly Reviews as well, they're actually not mutually exclusive.

Artifacts – Deliver (D3)

We have learned that there are four key areas that are core to creating an Agile PMO:

1. Know your **Program Velocity**. We call this "bandwidth." What is the current throughput of your project teams? How long does it take to do a project, on the average?
   a. If you do not know your Program Velocity, it will be difficult to do any kind of Program or Portfolio-level projections.
2. Do quarterly and annual **"cutting-room floor" exercises** where the projects included in a program and/or portfolio are prioritized by value-add.
   a. One PMO had to work with the Board of Directors, the Executives and Directors to cut 150 projects from a 250 project portfolio. The organization simply did not have the bandwidth to do everything to which it aspired.
   b. This is a very tough exercise to do, but the focus to the organization that it brings is massively valuable.

    c. It's not really possible to do this exercise if you do not know your team's bandwidth and/or velocity.

3. Sort the Project Teams into **dedicated Agile/ Scrum Teams**.

    a. Just like in any professional sport, you will want your teams working together on projects for one to two years at a time.

    b. A football coach seldom substitutes players during a game.

    c. In the same way, the project teams should not be revolving doors with people continually joining and exiting the project(s).

4. Put in place **Agile Governance**.

    a. This requires the organization to tailor how formal they would like their Agile Governance to be in order for it to work within the culture of the organization.

    b. The PMO will be taking project management templates away that the project and program managers either don't need or that were unnecessary documentation.

        i. One area that is problematic is Risk Management since traditional companies tend to spend too much time managing for risks that never materialize.

        ii. Agile is a superb risk management methdology since it only

> addresses, manages and mitigates risks that actually happen. If it doesn't occur, no time is wasted on excessive risk management.

c. The dasboard for reporting back to the Director, Executive and Board levels needs to be simple and straightforward and should include:

  i. The non-Gantt Gantt chart showing how the team's time has been allocated to which Programs, Products and/or Projects

  ii. Any resource exceptiions or contentions

  iii. Release burn-up charts for each Project and Program

  iv. A summary burn-up chart for each Portfolio

Once these four areas have been properly set-up, then the organization needs to be prepared to take years to measure, refine and adapt the PMO, Program and Portfolio levels.

For reporting purposes, the PMO should develop Release Burnup charts for use at the program level as well as the portfolio level (see Reporting section below in Chapter 9 for examples) and as mentioned, the templates to create those reports are made available to the project teams from the PMO. There are no additional artifacts needed for the Scrum of Scrums if your organization is using that as a tool for Program-level integration and cross dependency management. More is not necessarily better. Remember Nehimiah's trumpet? Keep it simple.

It is possible that your Program Managers that have the skill and experience may elect to create a combined Product Backlog (PBL) for use in helping the interdependent projects within a program prioritize dependencies and integration items. A Program Manager may elect to use a Scrum Board or a Kanban Board for Program level management. The Release Burnup Chart from the Scrum Board is used for reporting purposes on the combined PBL. This technique is optional for Program level use and currently is not part of traditional Scrum, but we have found it to be an effective tool within a Business Agile environment.

For traditional projects, the project reporting already in use will be used at the project level. For Portfolio reporting, the traditional projects are included in the "projects completed" Burnup charts that are used for the Agile Portfolio level reporting. This again allows a unified language approach to maintain clarity and alignment with organizational **Vision**, even though different project management methodologies may be used at the project level.

Chapter 7 Action Steps

1. Does your organization have a prioritization process at the Portfolio or Program level?
2. Write down, or draw, how your organization is structured for:
   c. Portfolio Management & Leadership

       d. Program Management

       e. Project Management

3. Compare your picture to the Stadium View shared in this chapter

    a. What changes will be necessary to move your PMO from a Traditional view to an Agile view?

    b. Is your organization prepared to invest the 5 to 7 years required to make the organizational and cultural changes that will be needed to go Agile?

    c. If not, why?

CHAPTER 8

RESOURCE MANAGEMENT – DELIVER (D3)

Resource Management – Deliver (D3)

Aligning resources can be very demanding in a Scrum environment. Some companies elect to group the Scrum teams and then dedicate (i.e. ring-fence) those teams for specific projects. This allows for projects to be moved to teams as bandwidth becomes available for the team. The teams stay together for longer stretches of time, moving from story to story and Sprint to Sprint as a team, so that they can better learn how each team member performs during a project.

Two additional tools can be used at the project level for Resource Management include. Those are:

- **Resource Allocation Timeline**. The Resource Allocation Timeline is the key report for this. An example of this is in section A below.

- **Project Costs**. If there is the need to do project cost accounting, then a very easy excel spreadsheet can be created to calculate the actual cost for any team member for any project and the PMO usually creates this template in Excel (i.e. team member * daily rate * number of days in Sprint * number of Sprints = team member project cost; plus add any other overhead, etc.) and then share that with the Project and Program leaders as needed.

For traditional projects, existing project reporting tools can be used and completed projects are then included in the Portfolio level reporting as shown below. The PMO should always reserve the right to introduce a method to create a Release Burnup chart for traditional projects, for example using the work packages completed in the WBS (work breakdown structure) and then reporting those for the Project, Program and Portfolio level on a monthly basis instead of on a Sprint basis.

Resource Allocations

The PMO (in cooperation with Product Development, Software Development, etc.) should do an exercise where all cross-functional team members needed to do the work have been allocated on a team-by-team basis. The Resource Allocation Timelines are a very quick way to review the "who" and the "what" for each Scrum team.

These timelines are updated monthly at the Portfolio Resource meetings.

By Team

For example, a New Product Development Program could be organized into the following Scrum teams:

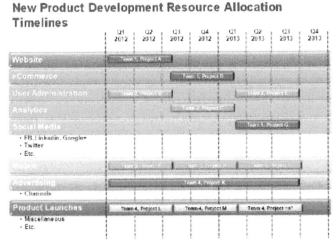

New Product Development Resource Allocation Timelines

Each Scrum team would mirror the Program's work streams. This allows a Program Manager to see which team is working on which project and when. This allows the Program Manager to track project completion velocity (i.e. the rate at which projects are completed). Not all projects are created equal, however, we have found that on larger Portfolios that (on the average) this is an accurate way to report results and progress towards the **Vision** and Goals.

Time Boxing

The Gantt chart above is used as the visual tool for the Portfolio leaders to manage project activity based upon the velocities within the projects and programs included in their portfolios. As adjustments are made based upon work completed, the remaining backlog items and downstream projects are then reprioritized.

The key thing to note is that there is a time box for each of the projects included in the work stream during which the team will be working on that project. Since the **Definition** of "done" has been aligned with Scrum, the promise made by the teams is that the most important items in the Product Backlog will be completed during the time box allotted. Scrum only makes commitments in two to four week increments.

The Scrum Team does not promise or commit to the overall scope of a project up front.

Especially since in Scrum environments it is expected that the Product Backlogs will grow during the course of a project, so an overall commitment for a project is outside the **Definition** of Scrum. In practice, however, a good team that has been working together for at least half a year should be able to have a realtively accurate 60 to 90 day "rolling view" of the work that is in the Product Backlog. Asking the team to commit to unknown unknowns six months out is simply a bad project management practice and shouldn't be done.

It is up to the Product Owner to determine if a minimum viable product (i.e. "MVP") has been achieved by the end of the time box and/or time allocated for the team for the project.

Chapter 8 Action Steps

1. To go Agile, your organization will most likely want to build-up experienced Agile talent from within the organization.
    a. Outline your organization's training, coaching and mentoring plan that internal candidates will go through to help them transform their thinking to become Agile.
2. Is your organization prepared to invest as much as $5,000, or more, per person to bring them up the learning curve on how to successfully implement Agile?
    a. If you need to bring in External Agile talent, are the hiring managers prepared to pay higher wages due the higher demand for top Agile talent?
    b. If not, why?
3. Is your organization prepared to change how it treats "date certain" types of projects that have hard deadlines?
    a. Write down how you can help your organization switch focus from the hard deadline to focusing on how long the team will be allocated to work on the project.

CHAPTER 9

REPORTING – DRIVE (D4)

Reporting – Drive (D4)

The PMO is usually responsible for creating the templates for the Burnup charts for each of the levels, Sprint, Project, Program and Portfolio and should introduce those as part of the overall Project Portfolio Management toolset for the organization's executive dashboard as outlined in Chapter 7.

All Scrum projects in the company most likely will want to use all four of these templates/reports while traditional projects will be included in the Program and Portfolio consolidated reporting (and will use traditional reporting methods for the project level).

The following are examples of the reporting for each level, Sprint, Project, Release and Portfolio.

Sprint Level Burnup or Burndown Charts

Sprint Burndown (or Burnup charts) will be used at the Project level and are for team use only. These should not be used for management purposes.

These charts are updated on a daily basis by the ScrumMaster and help the project team track their progress towards achieving the Sprint Goals.

The Project teams can choose to use points or hours when doing the Sprint Burndown chart. The next diagram is an example Sprint Burnup chart for a content database project where the team used points rather than hours, either method of using hours or points for Sprint reporting is acceptable (but, there is a growing body of research suggesting points are a superior way to forecast the size of the work involved):

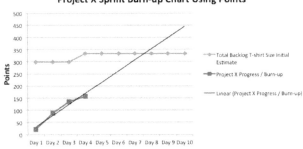

Project X Sprint Burn-up Chart Using Points

Project teams use Sprint Burnup (or Burndown) charts to help track their improvements Sprint-to-Sprint for both productivity and velocity. These charts are not intended for any kind of program management use.

Project Level Release Burnup Charts

The Project Release Burnup chart is a Sprint-by-Sprint report of the Scrum project's progress and is updated bi-weekly (latest a couple of days after the end of each Sprint) by the ScrumMaster. The next graph is an example Burnup chart, using points:

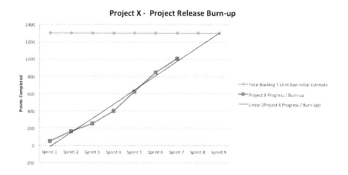

Program Level

The Release Burnup chart used at the Project level is the right one to use for Program management, reporting and corrective actions.

The trend line is a linear projection (i.e. forecast) of the project's progress vs. the amount of work left to be completed. This is a very useful view for the Program and Portfolio management teams to quickly see if a team needs additional help, mentoring or coaching or to view possible impacts on other Sprints within the project. For example, this helps the Program visualize if there are stories that are contingent upon other stories in another Sprint that are cross Program impacts and that need to be tracked and monitored.

An expanded version of this Burnup chart that can be created in Excel and used by the ScrumMaster to help the team improve their estimating activities Sprint-to-Sprint. The projects that are in-flight for a program can be quickly tracked using this type of report.

The Resource Allocation Timeline is configured in a Program view and is useful for Program Management. The Portfolio level report shown below can be created and used by the Program Managers to manage the Portfolio of Projects that they have in each of their Programs.

Portfolio Level

For the Portfolio level, we have two additional consolidated reports that will assist the Portfolio leaders and Program Managers in monitoring the progress of their portfolio, programs and all projects (both traditional and Agile). These reports are updated monthly by the PMO (and by the Portfolio/ Program owners) in time for the Portfolio's monthly priorities meeting.

The first Burnup chart is when you have multiple products supporting a single Program or Product:

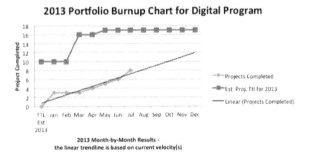

This shows the number of Projects completed within the Program (or Product) during the calendar year. The Backlog in this case is the number of projects that the Program (or Product) intends to complete during the year.

The grand finale for the Portfolio Manager is creating a consolidated overview of all projects included in the Prioritized Project Backlog for the Portfolio (all Programs and Projects together):

2012 Portfolio Total -
Burnup for all Digital Program Teams

This view gave the Portfolio owner the ability to see if their Portfolio was on track to achieve their objectives for 2012. Depending upon how the work is scheduled, there may have been more projects finishing in the second half of the year versus the first half of the year, but in general this will give the Portfolio leaders a good view into where they are currently at for the midpoint of 2012.

In the example above, the Portfolio was performing extremely well and had already achieved its target projects completed by the third quarter of the year and at the current velocity (i.e. rate of projects completed), assuming that the projects in the pipeline were of the same size/type as during the first three quarters of the year, they were on track to **Deliver** about 25% more during 2012 that what was **Delivered** in 2011. In 2013 they had already **Delivered** more that 60 projects by mid-year and were on track to **Deliver** over 120 projects for the year – a 100% increase over the 60 projects they completed in 2010 (so it only took 2½ years to double their throughput).

This is what Agile is all about and why even companies that used to be traditional in their thinking are discovering that this really is a better way to get things done and have more features or functions **Delivered**. The Portfolio Manager was relatively pleased with the results shared above, especially in light of the fact that this increase was achieved in the middle of transitioning the organization from traditional to Agile methodologies. In almost every other case we've seen (where a company transitions from traditional to Agile), there is usually a drop in productivity while the teams get used to using the new methodology. We believe that, in the case above, the PMOs tenacious focus on **Vision** allowed the transition to achieve these unusual and excellent results.

The key here is that it wasn't just doing the Agile training, launching and leaving, but rather taking the steps across the organization to prepare and implement the cultural changes necessary to enable such amazing performance in the middle of such a significant change. This brings us full circle back to where we started. For a PMO to succeed, they need to do the following five items:

1. Focus on **Vision**
2. Have clear **Definitions**
3. **Distill** clear **Agreements**
4. Have clear, short plans and time frames for **Delivery**
5. **Drive** success with frequent communication

The Portfolio Manager in this case, summed it up by observing, "We were not a mature PMO by any measure, particularly if you measured our PMO using a traditional Maturity Model Matrix, but we were a very effective PMO based on the business results achieved. It all really boiled down to having the right people, doing the right things, in the right way and at the right time." Using a simple framework combined with proper leadership will help achieve company goals and consistently **Deliver** value.

Chapter 9 Action Steps

1. Outline your organization's current reporting structure
   a. Compare that to the simplified dashboards shared in this chapter
   b. Identify how many of your reports will need to be eliminated in order to simplify your dashboards

2. Prepare your Executive and Board-level leadership for the change in the reports, at minimum, this should be part of a half-day Executive introduction to Business Agile.
    a. Best case would be that every Executive and Board member would go through the Business Agile Training.
3. If possible, the Executives and Board members should do the CSPO training as soon as possible.
    a. For example, one of the CTOs with which we worked balked at doing this for the first two years of a transformation. After going through the CSPO course himself, the CTO went back to the Executive and Board members and urged them all to invest the time in the 2-day CSPO course. We concur.

CHAPTER 10

STARTING YOUR JOURNEY TO AGILE

---

*"A journey of a thousand miles starts with a
single step." Lao Tzu (Laozi)*

A ny journey begins with the first step. Many
of the Business Agile techniques outlined in
this book may feel awkward or counter-intuitive.
But, they work. For the past two decades we have
used the Business Agile **UVF** in every kind of project,
management and leadership circumstance in the
US, Europe and Asia. When we have been able to be
involved from the beginning of a Project or Program,
we have had the same "wow" reaction to the out-
comes and results using the **UVF** that Nehemiah
experienced many years ago. It has been used effectively in a number of turn-around situations as well.
It simply works.

It works because it is methodology and culture
agnostic. In fact, it cuts across culture since it is

based on ancient, foundational Truth. While Tools and Technology have changed often during the past 5,000 years of human history, people really haven't changed. We recognize that there are variations from culture to culture, but people's behavior (on the average) is rather constant and consistent.

We started this book with **Vision**. We walked through the Project Management Continuum, Agile, Scrum, **VSPT**, the iterative **4D** and **4R Models**, the **1L + 1M + 1M = 1V** formula, **Cascading Vision**, the back story to Nehemiah, the **Agile Artifacts**, the Book of Nehemiah and how these Agile Artifacts were used. Finally, we laid out how to **Scale Agile** to the Enterprise level. We demonstrated the power of using **Vision** as the unifying force for your Products, Projects, Programs and Portfolios and how to use **Vision** to diffuse disagreement between Stakeholders.

Your organization's culture will be the biggest factor in whether or not you can successfully implement Agile with your teams. Corporate "antibodies" will most assuredly rise up and try to smother and kill off what they consider to be a virus. In many cases training, mentoring and coaching can help these "antibodies" be rehabilitated. But, we have found many cases where after every avenue for remedy has been exhausted that the only choice is to eliminate the "antibody." No organization can afford to have poisonous, cancerous "antibodies" continuously opposing the use of Agile and still expect the positive results that Agile, properly implemented, **Delivers**.

If you are going to embark on changing your organization from Waterfall/Traditional thinking to being Agile, we would strongly recommend that you find individuals that have successfully done this training, coaching and mentoring (hands-on) for other organizations. It is a very small pool of people that have actually done this in the world of Agile at the Portfolio and Program levels, since modern Agile is relatively new to the scene. You may need to look "under the rocks" inside your organization and find the individuals who have been successful, project after project as potential leaders and change agents for an Agile transformation (as well as at the Program and Portfolio levels). It will require intense investment in these leaders but they can become effective, trusted voices because of their cultural history.

These people are the ones that are most likely already either using Agile methods within your current structure or have understood Agile thinking and have been able to successfully implement it regardless of organizational constraints. These individuals have demonstrated a willingness to adapt and adjust to changing circumstances that is absolutely required for a successful transition to Agile.

If you do not have anyone internally that can become the Agile champion, then you will need to bring in skilled and experienced external people to assist. But, we are to the point where, after years of observation of what works and what doesn't work, that it should be mandatory for the Executive and Board levels go through Business Agile training before any Waterfall to Agile transformation commences.

One final thought, in "Flash Foresight," Dan Burrus pointed out that "Agility has been quite a buzzword lately in corporate circles. 'Customer needs are changing so fast,' goes the conventional wisdom, 'the competition and the marketplace are changing so fast, everything is changing so fast, that if you want to survive, you need be incredibly agile.'" Burrus goes on to state, however, "change has become simply too fast for even the best reaction time to be fast enough." By the time (a Tsunami wave) arrives, it's too late. It's certainly better to be Agile than Sluggish, but no amount of agility would have saved anyone from the Indian Ocean on December 26, 2004."[55]

If you're only trying to be merely Agile, you're already too late and becoming Agile is not enough. In the five to seven years it will take your organization to try to catch-up and become Agile, the companies that are already incredibly Agile will have already beaten you to the next thing. Make every effort to become more Agile but pay attention to the hard and soft trends in your organization and market so you can begin to become preactive as the Tsunami of change we currently live in begins to hit our shore.

The Nehemiah Effect has attempted to show you how ancient wisdom and foundational truths can cause successful results in today's environments. For a more recent example, no one thought there was oil or gas in Israel. However, an article in the Houston Chronicle reported that Yehezkeel Drukman documented the successful search for oil in gas in Israel this way, "the Biblical sources gave us the first indication of where to look. The rest was geology."[56]

Even though our world is changing at a faster and faster pace, we need to be looking at the future hard trends and certainties through the prism of the principles found in ancient wisdom. We believe there is more to learn from Nehemiah and other ancient writers. They will help us deal with the current and coming chaos caused by the speed at which everything is changing.

An old Japanese proverb states that we should, "slow down to go fast."

Our updated version of that proverb is to "look backward to move forward."

Nehemiah helps us do that and to him we say thanks. We also thank you for taking time to read our book and consider our ideas.

May all of your journeys
  be blessed,
  successful
May all
  of your projects
  result in a
  Nehemiah Effect

ACKNOWLEDGEMENTS

First and foremost, we would like to thank God and express our thanks and deepest gratitude to our wives, Claudia (Ted) and Gunilla (Andrew), our families, siblings and parents. Without you, this journey would have been meaningless.

We would like to thank and gratefully acknowledge the individuals with which we've worked, trained, coached and mentored during these past three decades. It is from all of you that we have **Distilled**, refined and honed the **UVF**.

To our Sunday School, Youth Group, Bible study teachers and leaders, along with the many Godly Professors and Pastors that we have had along the way, we would like to say thank you for helping shape us into men that understood the relevance, value and real-world application that the Bible still has for us today. It is an amazing treasure trove for business people that is still applicable for today.

We would like to express our many thanks to our wives, our sister Mary, and the small army of team members that helped proofread this book and for the excellent feedback they shared with us. We appreciate your time, input and encouragement to make this book even better.

Lastly, we would like to thank you, the reader for investing the time and effort in yourself and in becoming **Business Agile** using the **UVF**.

For more information about the co-authors, or about how to implement the Unified Vision Framework in your organization, see our website at www.nehemiaheffect.com, contact Andrew (akallman@andrewkallman. com, www.andrewkallman.com) and/or Ted (ted@unifiedvisiongroup.com, www.unified-visiongroup.com).

FOOTNOTES AND REFERENCES

1   http://www.vokeinc.com/
2   Dr. Jeff Sutherland in a blog post titled: "Tipping Point: Get Agile or Get Outsourced"
3   Source: http://www.agilemanifesto.org/
4   Source: http://www.agilemanifesto.org/principles.html
5   http://jeffsutherland.com/scrumhandbook.pdf
6   *Agile Product Management with Scrum,* page 27, Roman Pichler
7   Highsmith, 2009, 97
8   *Agile Product Management with Scrum,* page 27, Roman Pichler
9   Source: http://www.scrumalliance.org/pages/what_is_ scrum
10 Source: http://www.yoh.com/AboutYoh/PressRoom/Press% 20Releases/NewsItem?id=%7B9B8513C4-A6A6-4054- A8AD-9D59EA79FCDC%7D
11 Jim Collins, author of *Good to Great,* in 1992 on page 4 in his book *Beyond Entrepreneurship*
12 Jack Welch, former CEO of General Electric
13 Page 8 *"Understanding the Role of Vision in Project Success"* by Dale Christenson and Derek Walker in The Project Management Journal September of 2004.
14 Peter Drucker
15 Dr. Frank Luntz on page 134 in his book *Words that Work*
16 Daniel Burrus, in his book *Flash Foresight*

17 Max DePree, former CEO of Herman Miller, page 23 of his book *Leadership Jazz.*
18 Max DePree, again on page 130 of *"Leadership Jazz,"*
19 Jim Collins, on page 6 of *"Beyond Entrepreneurship"*
20 Page 31, "Good to Great," Jim Collins
21 Ibid.
22 Jack Welch,
23 Rudolph Flesch, PhD in his book *The Art of Clear Thinking*
24 Our thanks to Paul DeModica for this easy to remember "Distillation" from his book *Value Forward Selling.*
25 Proverbs 29:18
26 Proverbs 29:18
27 Proverbs 29:18
28 Proverbs 19:21
29 Proverbs 16:1
30 And, Proverbs 16:9
31 Psalm 127:1
32 Source: http://www.merriam-webster.com/dictionary/define
33 The definitions for **Distill, Deliver** and **Drive** are at following links:
      http://www.merriam-webster.com/dictionary/Distill
      http://www.merriam-webster.com/dictionary/Deliver
      http://www.merriam-webster.com/dictionary/Drive
34 See PMBOK Guide 5th Edition
35 For more on hearing the voice of God, see "Stark Raving Obedience: Radical Results from Listening Prayer" published in 2009 by Ted Kallman and Isaiah Kallman. You can order it from the website www.hearingGod.org.
36 Jim Collins in "Good to Great."
37 Daniel Burrus in his book *Flash Foresight*
38 The Project Management Institute Code of Ethics and Professional Conduct, http://www.pmi.org/About-Us/Ethics/~/media/PDF/Ethics/ap_pmicodeofethics.ashx
39 2 Timothy 3:16-17
40 Joshua 1:8
41 1 Kings 2:3
42 Matthew 6:9-13

43 Proverbs 23:7
44 Matthew 15:18-19
45 Luke 6:45
46 James 4:2
47 1 John 3:15
48 Matthew 5:28
49 Proverbs 4:23
50 Habakkuk 2:2
51 Matthew 5:37
52 2 Corinthians 1:17
53 James 1:8
54 Scrum Alliance Article on Scrum of Scrums (http://www. scrumalliance.org/articles/46-advice-on-conducting-the-scrum-of-scrums-meeting)
55 Page 42 of Dan Burrus' book "Flash Foresight"
56 Houston Chronicle (June 27, 1999)

CPSIA information can be obtained at www.ICGtesting.com
Printed in the USA
BVOW07s1310110615

404042BV00011B/54/P